HAUNTED
BIG BEND
FLORIDA

HAUNTED BIG BEND FLORIDA

ALAN BROWN

HAUNTED
AMERICA

Published by Haunted America
A Division of The History Press
Charleston, SC 29403
www.historypress.net

Unless otherwise noted, all images appear courtesy of the author.

First published 2013

ISBN 978.1.5402.3229.8

Library of Congress CIP data applied for.

To Owen Cole Walker,
the newest addition to our family.

CONTENTS

CONTENTS

ACKNOWLEDGEMENTS

A number of individuals have made invaluable contributions to the writing of this book. I am particularly indebted to previous works that have been written about Florida's Panhandle, including *Haunted Monticello, Florida*, by Betty Davis and the Big Bend Ghost Trackers; *Hauntings in Florida's Panhandle*, by Nicole Carlson Easley; *Florida's Ghostly Legends and Haunted Folklore*, by Greg Jenkins; and *Haunting Sunshine*, by Jack Powell. The folklore studies conducted by Dale Cox have also enhanced the quality of this book.

This writer would also like to acknowledge the contributions of two of the ghost tours in this area: Big Bend Ghost Trackers of Monticello and the Historic Ghost Tours of Tallahassee. Not only have they exposed thousands of visitors to the Big Bend's haunted sites, but they also make impressive annual contributions to area charities. Walking tours such as these add a positive luster to the paranormal field.

Finally, I am grateful to those people who assisted me on a personal level with the writing of this book. The people who happily shared their time and stories with me helped to distinguish this book from previously published works. I would also like to thank the University Research Committee for awarding me the grant money that funded my ghost-story collecting trip to the Big Bend. Of course, I counted on the professionalism of the staff of The History Press to assist me with creating a quality product. Most of all, I would like to thank my wife, Marilyn, on whose judgment and encouragement I have grown to depend.

Introduction

The Big Bend of Florida is an informal name given to a section of the counties in the Florida Panhandle. According to geologists, the Big Bend includes that part of Florida's coastline that is bounded by the mouth of the Apalachicola River and the Central Barrier Coast in Southwest Florida. Counties existing within Florida's Big Bend are generally considered to be Gadsden County, Dixie County, Liberty County, Wakulla County, Jefferson County, Madison County, Franklin County, Taylor County and Leon County. The largest cities in this region are Tallahassee, Apalachicola and Panama City.

The Big Bend of Florida is sometimes referred to as Florida's Forgotten Coast, a registered trademark coined by the Apalachicola Chamber of Commerce in the early 1990s. This term is essentially an appeal to entrepreneurs to set up business in this relatively undeveloped section of coastline. It also stems from the fact that many of this area's natural wonders—such as Simmons Bayou, St. James Island and St. Marks Lighthouse and nature preserve—have not yet been discovered by the thousands of tourists who visit Florida every year.

Florida's Big Bend does not deserve to be forgotten. It includes a number of beautiful state parks and wildlife preserves, such as St. Joseph's Peninsula State Park, St. Vincent National Wildlife Refuge, Wakulla State Forest, Bald Point State Park and Tate's Hell State Forest. The Big Bend also contains sites that would be of interest to history buffs. Fans of the paranormal should take the time and trouble to visit the Big Bend as well because many of these historical sites are reputed to be haunted. In fact, one of the cities in the Big Bend—Monticello—is said to be one of the most haunted cities in the entire Southeast. Although several of the Big Bend's ghost stories had been published before, they had been published together in a single volume. During our trip to the Big Bend in October 2012, my wife, Marilyn, and I visited haunted sites in Apalachicola, Monticello, Quincy and Tallahassee. We also spent the night in several haunted bed-and-breakfasts, toured several historic homes and took ghost tours in Monticello and Tallahassee. My primary purpose in writing this book was to give exposure to the area's rich body of ghost lore, which, hopefully, will never be forgotten by those who read *Haunted Big Bend, Florida*.

1
APALACHICOLA

COOMBS INN

James Nathaniel Coombs was Apalachicola's most prosperous businessmen in the late 1800s and the early 1900s. He was born in Old Town, Maine, on August 15, 1847. As a boy, he learned about the lumber business from his father, who ran a lumber mill. After graduating from the public schools, James served as a sergeant in the Twenty-eighth Maine Volunteer Infantry Regiment during the Civil War. In 1866, he married Maria A. Starrett, his childhood sweetheart.

Coombs moved to Pensacola in 1870, where he decided to try his hand at the lumber business, just as his father had. He was one of the first businessmen in Florida to appreciate the value of yellow pine lumber. In 1877, Coombs moved to Apalachicola, where he acquired the Sunny South sawmill. In 1878, Apalachicola was becoming known statewide as a lumber depot, primarily because of Coombs's business interests. By 1909, he had become president of the Franklin County Lumber Company of Carrabelle, president of the First National Bank and president of the Coombs Company, which exported pine and cypress lumber. While living in Apalachicola, he became very active in the Republican Party, serving as the delegate to the Republican National Convention from Florida in 1896. He was also a member of the Republican National Committee from Florida between 1907 and 1908. Legend has it that Theodore Roosevelt, whom he had met at the Republican National convention, offered him the position of vice

James N. Coombs, a wealthy entrepreneur, built this private residence in 1904.

president in 1905, but Coombs turned him down because the salary was not high enough. Coombs was also a member of several social organizations, including the Order of Elks, the Knights of Pythias and the Masonic Order.

In 1904, James N. Coombs decided it was time to build a house suitable for a man of his prominence. George H. Marshall, a local architect, was hired to design Coombs's new house. Like most of the Queen Anne–style homes Marshall had constructed in Apalachicola, the Coombs house had wooden floors and ceilings, a wrap-around veranda, a widow's walk and an open balcony on the second floor. For the next few years, Coombs and his wife enjoyed the splendor of their new home. However, he suffered a dramatic reversal of fortune in 1911. On March 6, the attic of his beautiful home at 80 Sixth Street caught fire. By the time the fire wagons arrived, the flames had burned through the roof. The firemen pulled out their fire hoses and immediately began dousing the fire. The house, although severely damaged by fire and water, was spared. However, most of Mrs. Coombs's furniture, linens and china were destroyed. For the next few days, the Franklin Hotel became the couple's new home. Ten days after the devastating fire, Marie died in the hotel. Her husband followed her in death on April 8, 1911.

The Coombs house was occupied by members of the Coombs family for the next fifty years. By the 1960s, the once stately Coombs House was boarded up and dilapidated. Vandals had inflicted heavy damage on the old house. During this period of neglect, the back balcony collapsed to the ground below. In 1978, the old house was on the verge of being condemned when Lynn Wilson, an interior decorator, and her husband, Bill Spohrer, visited Apalachicola and drove past the once fine mansion. Impressed with the house's potential, she and her husband tracked down the owners and purchased it. The couple immediately set about restoring the Coombs house with local carpenters and painters. The workmen added eleven bathrooms and installed a modern breakfast kitchen. In 1994, the house began operating as a bed-and-breakfast. Some people believe that the antique furnishings, the four-poster beds and the polished hardwood floors have made the old home so inviting that the original owners have returned.

Most of the haunted activity in the Combs House Inn takes place in Room Number 8, the Coombs Suite. In her book *Hauntings in Florida's Panhandle*, author Nicole Carlson Easley says that several female guests staying in the Coombs Suite have felt a male hand stroking their cheek during the night. Ron Jackson, the editor and publisher of *Domain Name Journal*, stayed in the Coombs Suite. During the night, he was awakened by the sound of a water bottle falling on the floor. His first thought was that his wife, Diana, had gotten up to go to the bathroom and accidentally knocked the water bottle off the top of the compact refrigerator near his bed. However, when he looked over at the refrigerator, the water bottle was still sitting where he had left it. Something told him to climb out of bed and touch the bottle. When he did, he was shocked to find that the water bottle that had been sitting outside of the refrigerator for several hours was still ice cold. Careful not to wake up his wife, Jackson slipped back into bed and went back to sleep. When he awoke the next morning, he noticed that the water bottle was still on top of the refrigerator and that another water bottle was lying on the floor. Diana told him that she had taken a bottle of water out of the refrigerator during the night and placed it on the refrigerator. However, neither of them could explain how the first water bottle fell on the floor when no one was walking around the room.

According to Chad Lewis and Terry Fisk, the authors of *The Florida Road Guide to Haunted Locations*, Rooms Number 6 (The Raney Room) and Number 7 (the Fisk Room) are said to be haunted by the ghosts of the children who slept there. Guests and employees have walked through cold spots in these rooms. The ghostly giggles of small children have been heard inside the rooms when no one is there. The echoes of childish laughter occasionally make their way down the staircase to the parlor. Desk clerks have often heard the ghostly voices of children in the lobby.

The apparitions of adult males have also made an appearance inside the bed-and-breakfast. One of the employees of the inn saw a carpenter walk down the staircase late one evening and vanish. The ghostly workman has also been sighted working on the hinges of a door in one of the rooms on the first floor. A guest who was staring out of a dining room window saw the ghost of Mr. Coombs standing on the deck, taking in the scenery. A few seconds later, he walked through a wall where there used to be a door. Coombs's ghost has also been seen walking from the dining room into a guest room on the first floor.

A female spirit is also said to have taken up residence in the Coombs House. According to Nicole Carlson Easley, a woman wearing a long, flowing gown walked past a guest standing in the parlor. She disappeared when he turned around to speak to her. A female employee told Chad Lewis

A spectral woman wearing a nineteenth-century gown walked past a guest in the parlor.

and Terry Fisk that a gentleman had just walked up the stairs to the attic when, out of the corner of his eye, he saw an older woman and a younger woman standing side by side. When the gentleman turned his head for a better look, they were gone.

Lynn Wilson and Bill Spohrer have expanded the bed-and-breakfast since it first opened in 1994. In 1998, the couple purchased a large, old house a block away. They restored the 1911 home and named it "Coombs Villas." Weddings and meetings are held in the renovated carriage house. In 2007, they bought the house next door that Coombs had built for his mother and his aunt and converted it into four luxury suites. However, only the Coombs House appears to be haunted, probably because this is the only place that the Coombs family called home.

THE ORMAN HOUSE

Thomas Orman was born in 1799 in Salina, New York. When he was eighteen years old, he traveled down the Mississippi River on a barge to New Orleans. For the next year, he worked on a sugar plantation. He then partnered with Cyrus Young and moved to Florida, where they set up one of the state's first salt works. While he was living in Webbville, Florida, Orman married a widow named Sarah Love Trippe, who hailed from a prominent family. In 1830, the couple's only child, William Thomas Orman, was born. After the plan to make Webbville the county seat fell through, Orman moved his family south down the Apalachicola River. Orman started a cotton plantation twelve miles north of Apalachicola, not far from the Alabama border. In 1834, he set up a mercantile store and cotton warehouse, and by 1843, he owned eleven of the forty-three cotton warehouses in Apalachicola. He made a fortune buying cotton as it was transported down the river to Apalachicola and selling it to markets in Europe and in the northern United States. He became one of three men in town who owned two hundred slaves or more.

In 1836, Orman decided that it was time to build a house that would accommodate his six-foot-seven-inch frame and reflect his wealth and status. He decided to build his mansion on a bluff overlooking the Apalachicola River. The walls, windows, doors and trim were cut to measure in Syracuse, New York, and floated down the river to Apalachicola. The framework of the house was made of cypress that was cut in and around Apalachicola.

Visitors have heard phantom footsteps and the rattling of doorknobs in the Orman House.

The floors, made of heart pine, are termite resistant because of their high resin content, which, unfortunately, also makes them highly flammable. The steps in the front of the house were carved from granite quarried in Quincy, Massachusetts. The doorways were made extra high so that Orman could pass through them without bumping his head. When construction of the house was completed in 1838, it became one of the showplaces of Apalachicola, even though it had only four rooms: a dining room, a parlor and two upstairs bedrooms. Guests who attended the Ormans' lavish parties include such luminaries as Robert E. Lee, botanist Dr. Alvin Wentworth Chapman and Dr. John Corrie, the inventor of mechanical refrigeration.

In the years preceding the Civil War, Orman set about to increase his land holdings. In 1857, he developed the 259-acre Owl Creek plantation twenty-two miles upriver from Apalachicola. In 1861, Orman purchased St. George Island at thirty cents per acre. During the Civil War, he was arrested by the Union army for allegedly murdering a Union sympathizer and by the Confederate army on the charge of being a Union spy. He was found not guilty on both charges. Thomas Orman continued working as a cotton merchant well into the 1870s. He died in 1880.

Thomas Orman's son, William Thomas, became his sole heir. Just before the Civil War, William graduated from Yale with a law degree. He was one of the first young men to enlist in the Confederate army in 1861. For much of the war, he served as commander of a gunboat named the *Bradford*. Later, he achieved the rank of lieutenant in the Confederate army, participating in such fierce battles as Shiloh and Stones River.

William Orman returned home in 1865. The next year, the six-foot-five-inch William married Anna V. Smith of Mount Pleasant. Sara Genevieve Orman was their only child. In the years following the Civil War, William Orman ventured into real estate and politics. He was eventually elected as a two-term congressman from the state of Florida. He and his wife took possession of the house after Thomas Orman died in 1880. In 1895, the three buildings in the back were added together to form a single-story addition to the house.

William's daughter, known by the nickname "Sadie," married Judge John Fennimore Cooper Griggs, who was appointed customs agent for the state of Florida. After living in Jacksonville and Tampa for a few years, the couple moved to Apalachicola in 1921. The judge added the library, which served as his chambers. He also had a door leading from the porch to his chambers for the convenience of his clients.

The mansion remained in the Orman family for 156 years. In 1994, Anna and Douglas Caidy purchased the dilapidated old mansion. The couple renovated the Orman House and converted it into a bed-and-breakfast. They named it "Magnolia Hall" after the magnolia trees that Thomas Orman planted in the yard. Five years later, the Florida State parks division bought the historic home.

Like many antebellum mansions, Thomas Orman's former home is the focus of a number of legends. The best-known of these tales concerns Thomas Orman's wife, Sarah. The story goes that after Apalachicola was captured by the Union army in 1862, Sarah started placing a keg of nails on the widow's walk of the mansion, ostensibly for repairs to the roof. Actually, though, she used the nail keg to signal to the town that the Yankees were in town. Other people say that she used the nail keg to warn Confederate soldiers who had returned to Apalachicola on furlough or to announce to the town that Thomas Orman was ready to trade in cotton. Some people say that Sarah Orman's ghost is still walking around the widow's walk. Apparently, she is still eager to warn the locals.

Other types of ghostly activity have also been reported at the Orman House over the years. Many people passing through the house have heard phantom footsteps on the stairs and rattling doorknobs. Members of a ghost-hunting group that set up their equipment in the attic and the porch captured orbs on their cameras and disembodied voices on their digital voice recorders. People have also smelled the distinctive odor of gunpowder inside the house and seen ghostly Union soldiers standing in the yard. In their book *The Florida Road Guide to Haunted Locations,* authors Chad Lewis and Terry Fisk tell the story of the wife of one of the painters who was working in the house. She was standing in one of the rooms when she saw a woman walk down the hallway. She realized that she had had an encounter with the paranormal when she followed the woman into one of the rooms and discovered that she was alone. On another occasion, a visitor to the mansion proclaimed that he did not believe in ghosts and that the Orman House was definitely not haunted. He was walking down the stairs when suddenly he felt someone push him from behind, causing him to lose his balance and fall down the stairs. When he turned around, he was preparing to yell at the practical joker who could have seriously injured him. As soon as he discovered that no one was walking behind him, he dashed out of the house and never came back.

The best source of information about the Orman House, including its ghost stories, is Ranger Mike Kinnett. Mike said that on October 18, 2012, he was guiding a medium from Clearwater, Florida, around the house. After the tour, she asked Mike if he believed in reincarnation: "I'm picking up that you are reincarnated from one of the workers who worked for the company that built this house. That's how come you know so much about it. You're related to someone who was actually working here at that time." Mike would be the first to admit that he gained his knowledge about the Orman house the conventional way: through extensive research.

A few months earlier, a man who dated one of the descendants of the Orman family told Mike that one morning, he was returning home from the night shift at a paper company when he stopped by the Orman House, which was empty at the time. He decided to test the veracity of a rumor he had heard about a small table that sat between two of the windows in the parlor. According to the legend, if the table is moved anywhere in the house, it will return to its original place in the parlor within an hour. He placed the table in a bedroom and waited. Thirty minutes later, the table slid back and forth across the floor. "He said he didn't know if he should be elated because he had found proof of paranormal activity or run out of the house screaming," Mike said.

The same man told Mike about a terrifying experience two of his grandsons had in the old house. On their way back home from school, they

If this table is removed from its proper place in the parlor, it will return to its original position within one hour.

decided to walk through the back door leading into the parlor. When they looked upstairs, they were horrified to see two apparitions standing on the stairs. The boys ran four blocks to a friend's house and told him about seeing two strange figures dressed in 1800s period clothing walking down the stairs.

Ranger Mike credits the fact that he has had very few experiences with the uncanny inside the house where he has worked for so long because of his close relationship with the ghosts. "People who are really in touch with the spirit world tell me that it is because the Ormans' ancestors like me," Mike said. "If they didn't, I'd have more paranormal activity inside the house."

THE GIBSON INN

The Gibson Inn was built by Fulton Buck of black cypress and heart pine in 1907 in the Florida "Cracker" architectural style. The distinctive features of the inn originally known as the Franklin Hotel include raised floors, high ceilings

The Gibson Inn, which was built in 1907, is haunted by Captain Wood, who died in Room 309.

and wrap-around verandas. Perched on top of the roof are a cupola and widow's walk. In 1922, the Gibson sisters—Mary Ellen "Sunshine" Gibson and Annie Gibson Hays—purchased the inn. Annie's son, Pat Hays, and his family assisted with operating and upgrading the hotel. After Annie remarried and moved to Tallahassee in 1925, her son Edward and his wife, Kathleen, ran the Gibson Hotel with his Aunt "Sunshine." Between 1929 and 1934, Works Progress Administration workers were hired to construct the Chapman Auditorium. Between 1942 and 1945, the U.S. Army took over the Gibson Inn and converted it into an officers' club and a hotel for the families of soldiers awaiting transfer from Camp Gordon Johnson. While their hotel was commandeered by the army, the Hays family resided in the Buck House behind the inn. After the Hays family sold the Gibson Inn in 1945, it was run by a number of different owners over the years. In 1977, the state declared the old run-down hotel a fire hazard and closed it down. The next year, it was purchased by a man who operated it as a pool hall and bar. In 1983, architects Dave Fronczack and Rick B. Arnett were hired by Michael and Neil Koun and Michael Merlo to renovate the hotel. The proud old inn was completely restored at a cost of $1.2 million and reopened on November 1, 1986.

Members of the hotel staff have been regaling visitors and ghost hunters with stories of the Gibson Inn's haunted past for many years. One of the most persistent ghost legends involves an old woman who sits in a rocking chair in the cupola. However, there are two serious problems with this story. First of all, no rocking chair has ever sat up in the cupola. The fact that the cupola is always locked enhances the supernatural aspect of the tale even more.

Many stories have been told about the widow's walk as well. People staying just below the widow's walk have heard a woman's footsteps above them. They said that the woman seemed to be walking back and forth on the widow's walk, almost as if she trying to catch sight of a ship in the ocean.

One of the night clerks is convinced that the dining room is haunted. On at least two occasions, she has seen a black shape move across the entranceway to the dining room. In September 2012, she was doing the night audits at 7:00 a.m. at her desk in the lobby when she heard an unnerving sound coming from the bar area in the dining room. "I heard something like a woman crying," she said. "I thought that maybe somebody left the TV on, so I walked into the bar, and there was nothing turned on. So I came back to the front desk, thinking that maybe it was a cat outside or whatever. But then I heard it again. It was like sobbing. So I walked into the bar, and it got louder. But when I walked around the bar, there was nobody there. It definitely sounded like a woman sobbing."

This particular employee has also had a strange experience in the parlor. "There's a fake chandelier by the piano in the parlor. When we come in, we turn it on. We turn it off when we leave. But when we come in and the chandelier is on, that's when the hairs on the head start to stand up."

One of the ghosts that haunt the bar is thought to be the spirit of a young WPA worker. Every Saturday night between 1929 and 1934, he entertained guests with his virtuoso piano playing. Some employees of the Gibson Inn believe that he enjoyed playing there so much that he is still on the job. Sometimes they hear phantom footsteps and the sound of the piano playing when no one else is around.

Hotels and bed-and-breakfasts that have acquired haunted reputations frequently attract guests who are staying there in the hope of having some sort of supernatural encounter. One night, a woman who announced that she was a medium was speaking to the night clerk at the front desk. "She was just talking away about different places she's stayed at and weird things that have happened to her," the clerk said. All of a sudden, she stopped talking to the night clerk and began talking to someone who was not there. She seemed to have entered a different "zone." After a minute or so, she turned back to the night clerk and said, "Oh, that was somebody's uncle. He was going on about his arthritis." Apparently, the "uncle" she was conferring with was the spirit of someone who had either worked at the Gibson Inn or who had stayed there years ago.

Two of the spirits roaming the old inn have been identified. One of them is the ghost of Captain Wood, a regular guest at the Gibson Inn who died of pneumonia in Room 309, despite Sunshine's best efforts to save him. He always stayed in this particular room when he visited Apalachicola because it afforded him a good view of his ship. Most guests who have felt his presence say that he is a mischievous spirit. People staying in the room who have tried to charge their cellphones in the morning have discovered that someone— or something—unplugged them during the night. Lights tend to go on and off by themselves in that room as well. Captain Wood is especially fond of taunting visitors by moving objects around while they are asleep or out of their rooms. One of the night clerks said that in 2010, a woman asked her to move things around in Room 309 while she and her husband went to dinner. "She wanted to fool her husband into thinking there was a ghost in her room," the clerk said. "So I took three pairs of shoes on the floor to make it look like someone had been walking in them. I also put the toilet seat down and placed a wine glass on top of the lid. When they returned from dinner, the wife talked to me at the front desk while her husband went upstairs and took pictures. He was trying to photograph Captain Wood's ghost. A few minutes later, he came down the stairs and showed us one of the pictures he had taken. There was an orb, I guess you call it, right over the shoes. I guess this was Captain Wood's way of saying, 'You can play around all you want, but I'm still here.'" The apparition of Captain Wood, which has appeared to only a few "lucky" individuals, usually manifests itself as a small man wearing blue pants and a jacket.

Apparently, Captain Wood's ghost enjoys getting up close and personal with some of the guests staying in his room. In their book *The Florida Road Guide to Haunted Locations*, authors Chad Lewis and Terry Fisk cites instances where people were touched on the shoulder or even pinched on the behind in the room. A few people who have spent the night in Room 309 report that invisible hands pulled the covers up to their neck while they were asleep. A couple had fallen asleep when they were awakened by someone violently shaking their bed. A woman who had just checked in was unpacking her suitcase on the bed. She went downstairs to the lobby to talk to the desk clerk, and when she returned to Room 309, she was shocked to find her suitcase sitting on the floor by the bed. All of the clothes that she had laid on the bed were neatly stacked inside.

The other ghost whose name is known is the spirit of Sunshine Gibson. She typically manifests herself as a woman in a long gray dress with her hair pulled back in a bun, and she usually walks around the second floor. Occasionally, the spectral figure of the "woman in gray" is seen walking down the stairs and into the bar. A few minutes later, she leaves the bar and walks back up the stairs. She has also been seen walking down the hallway with a serious, preoccupied look on her face. Some witnesses say that she appears to be making sure that things are running smoothly. Sunshine's ghost is also said to call up the night clerks sitting at the front desk. The calls frequently come from empty guest rooms or from the kitchen phone, which has not been working for some time. The speaker on the phone has turned on by itself as well. One night, a call came from the manager's office. Goosebumps rose up the night clerk's arms when she realized that the manager had left the inn two hours earlier. The night clerks can tell when Sunshine has called them up because the only sound they hear on the other end of the line is a crackling noise.

A few nameless ghosts show up occasionally as well. According to Chad Lewis and Terry Fisk, guests have seen a well-dressed man wearing a dark suit and a top hat walking down the hallway. He is usually carrying a black suitcase. Witnesses say that the quiet, determined-looking man slowly dissipates as he reaches the end of the hallway. The spirits of soldiers wearing the khaki green uniforms of the World War II era have been sighted milling around outside the restaurant. They vanish whenever anyone tries talking to them.

Not surprisingly, working at the Gibson Inn is rarely boring. However, despite the high amount of paranormal activity that regularly occurs in the old inn, none of the employees are afraid to work there. Most of them become, at the very least, more open-minded regarding the possibility that the hotel is haunted. A few of them become strong believers in the paranormal, like the desk clerk who said, "I am certain that there are still spirits in the house. I really am."

2
CHIPLEY

GHOST OF THE LIME SINK

Sinkholes are as integral a part of the Florida landscape as palmetto fronds and palm trees. Sinkholes are created when rainfall absorbs acids from decaying plants. The water then filters into the ground and slowly dissolves the limestone underneath, forming voids and cavities. Eventually, more water enters and enlarges these spaces, creating large caverns. Sinkholes are produced when the land surface above collapses into the cavities. Sinkholes are a naturally occurring phenomenon that can be caused by heavy rains after severe droughts. However, human beings can inadvertently create sinkholes by drilling new wills, creating artificial ponds or withdrawing too much groundwater. Most sinkholes are no more than ten to twelve feet in diameter. Around the turn of the century, a giant sinkhole in Chipley, Florida, was responsible for one of the area's best-known ghost stories.

In his book *Washington—Florida's Twelfth County*, author E.W. Carswell recounts the story of a group of teenagers and their ill-fated trip to the Lime Sink, which at the time was on property owned by Captain Angus McMillan. Members of the group included McMillan's eighteen-year-old daughter, Neta; fourteen-year-old Nannie Callaway; and eighteen-year-old Graymore Pridgeon. Apparently, the two girls were wading in the water when they fell into a thirty-foot chasm under the water. Because neither girl could swim, they began thrashing around in the water, screaming. Neta's fourteen-year-old brother, Jeff, was working in a field nearby when he heard the girls' cries for help. He dove into Lime Sink and dragged Graymore out of the water. Unfortunately, he was unable to save Neta and Nannie.

Word of the tragedy spread like wildfire through the small community. Residents from Chipley rushed to the scene and immediately initiated a search-and-rescue operation. Using a grappling hook, the men were able to retrieve Nannie's body. A few days later, a diver from Pensacola was summoned to Lime Sink. He explored the depths of the sinkhole but was unable to locate Neta's body. He speculated that her corpse might have floated into one of the area's underwater caverns. After an attempt to pump all of the water out of Lime Sink failed, rescuers gave up the search for Neta McMillan's body. To this day, its location is a mystery.

As often happens in cases like this, a ghost story emerged to keep the memory of Neta McMillan alive. The story goes that on foggy nights, a female apparition can be seen walking on the surface of the waters of Lime Sink. According to folklore, Neta McMillan's spirit will never truly find rest until her body is found and she receives a Christian burial. Lime Sink is now on private property, so curiosity seekers are advised to keep their distance out of respect for the law and for the dear departed.

3
FRANKLIN COUNTY

TATE'S HELL STATE FOREST

Tate's Hell State Forest is composed of 202,437 acres of land in Franklin County, just south of Apalachicola National Forest. This huge tract of land once supported twelve major community types: wet flatwoods, baygall, seepage slope, wet prairie, basin swamp, floodplain forest, upland hardwood forest, floodplain swamp, scrub, pine ridges, sandhill and dense thickets. Between the 1950s and the early 1990s, this area was sold for timber production. During this forty-year period, this invaluable natural resource incurred an extensive loss of wildlife and habitat through the construction of eight thousand miles of logging roads and the digging of long drainage canals. The original plants and trees were replaced with large stands of slash pine fertilized with nitrogen and phosphorus. In 1994, the entire area was acquired by the State of Florida, which has undertaken a massive restoration project to protect the Apalachicola Bay from severe freshwater run-off. Today, Tate's Hell State Forest is home to a number of endangered plants (like Chapman's butterwort and Florida bear grass), animals (the gopher tortoise and American black bear, among them) and birds (such as the bald eagle and red-cockaded woodpecker). The forest's primary hydrologic feature, Tate's Hell Swamp, is also its most mysterious.

Tate's Hell State Forest derives its name from Cebe Tate, a local farmer who ventured into the swamp in 1875 in search of a panther that had been killing his livestock. Accompanied only by his dogs and armed with just a shotgun, he soon became disoriented in the dense undergrowth. For seven days, he wandered through the forest, drinking swamp water and subsisting on roots and berries. By the time he staggered into a clearing near Carrabelle, he had been bitten by snakes and was nearly starved to death. His brown beard had turned snow white. The story goes that after uttering the words, "My name is Cebe Tate, and I just came from Hell," he dropped dead. Cebe Tate survived this ordeal much longer than a lesser man would have.

Even though Tate's Hell State Forest's thirty-five miles of streams, creeks and rivers offer tourists excellent canoeing, boating and fishing, it still projects a somewhat foreboding aura. In the 1970s, visitors began reporting sightings of a Big Foot–like creature called the Skunk Ape. A plaster cast made of one of the creature's tracks in the 1980s suggested that it weighed over five hundred pounds. Shimmering spirits have been seen flitting through the forest as well. One wonders if one of these ghost lights could be the restless spirit of Cebe Taylor, still trying to find a way out of "Hell." Another possibility could be that whatever scared Cebe Taylor enough to turn his beard completely white is still roaming around in darkest regions of the forest.

4

GADSDEN COUNTY

McLANE INDIAN MASSACRE SITE

John McLane was born in Savannah, Georgia, in 1820. Six years later, he arrived in Florida with his mother, Nancy, and stepfather. They settled a few miles north of Quincy. In 1837, the family moved to a new area sixteen miles southwest of Quincy. John's stepfather cleared a plot of land and built a log cabin, twelve by fifteen feet. For the most part, the McLane family was completely isolated. In fact, their nearest white neighbor lived four miles away to the east.

It soon became clear that John McLane's stepfather had underestimated the perils of living in such a sparsely settled region. By 1840, relations between whites and Chief Pascofa's band of Creek Indians were becoming strained. Fort Yates was built at Estiffanulga after a series of Indian attacks in 1839. Fort Yates was soon abandoned, and a blockhouse, Fort Preston, was built at Bristol, along with two other near Wakulla Spring and the St. Marks River. In late January 1840, a war party of twenty to thirty Creeks intercepted a wagon carrying supplies and provisions to Fort Preston on the old Federal Road. The Indians drove off the three guards and set the wagon afire. Captain Bullock and his company of dragoons pursued the Indians but failed to apprehend them.

Shortly after the troops withdrew, Pascofa's warriors made their way to the McLane homestead. On April 23, 1840, John McLane's stepfather was in Quincy, leaving John's thirteen-year-old sister, Katharine; his two-year-old sister; and the baby in his and his mother's care. At sunrise, John's mother sent him to the field to pick some herbs for tea. Meanwhile, his sister was in the cow pen milking a cow. John was walking between the house and the cow pen when he heard a low rustling sound in the bushes northwest of the house. At first, he thought some of the cattle were running to the pen. However, when he turned around, John was shocked to see a band of eighteen Creek Indians running toward the house. The Indians, armed with guns, bows and arrows and scalping knives, were clearly intent upon murdering all of the occupants of the cabin. John screamed to his sister to run to the house as fast as she could. John followed her, but before he could reach the house, a warrior fired his rifle, grazing John in his left shoulder. With his shoulder throbbing, John dashed inside the house and fastened the latch. Peering out through one of the holes his stepfather had made in the logs for defense, John watched the Creeks as they entered the outside kitchen and helped themselves to the family's food stores.

Staring in horror at the Indians in the kitchen, John's mother decided to escape from the cabin with her children. She told John that she would take the older girl and the two younger children east to the Pickett or McDougal settlements four miles away. Kissing John goodbye, his mother helped the children through the window and then climbed out herself. Looking through one of the loop-holes, John saw two Creeks trying to head off his mother and siblings from the north. John opened the front door and took aim with his rifle at one of the Indians, but before he could get off a shot, a rifle ball whistled past his ear, forcing him back into the house. Tears streamed down his face as he listened helplessly to the screams of his family. The Indians shot his mother in the forehead and Katherine in the head. They brained the two little ones in the head with a lightwood knot.

John was trying to take in the full horror of the scene when he was distracted by the smell of burning wood. He turned his head and noticed that the Creeks had set fire to the kitchen in the hopes that the flames would spread to the house, which was only fifteen feet away. The Creeks ignited balls of cotton they had found in the workshop and tossed them on top of the house, but the roof was so steep that they rolled off harmlessly. Peering through a hole, John observed an Indian with bow in hand trying to sneak around the east side of the cabin while his companions tried to distract John by making a lot of racket on the west side. John focused his attention on the solitary Indian creeping up to the east side of the cabin. When the Indian was twenty feet from the cabin, John fired his musket, mortally wounding him in the bowels. The Indian's friends dragged his wounded body to safety, but John could tell by all the wailing and chanting that he had killed a person of importance.

In the middle of the afternoon of the same day, John was looking through the hole on the north side of the house when he saw his stepfather ride up with the mare and cart. John rushed out of the house and breathlessly told him of the murder of his mother and three siblings. His stepfather told John to take the mare and ride to the nearest settlement while he avenged the deaths of his wife and children. Unable to dissuade his stepfather from his foolhardy plan, John mounted the mare and headed off through the piney woods. Several Creeks pursued him, but John quickly outdistanced them. At dusk, John reached the McDougal and Pickett settlement on the east. During the night, his stepfather arrived. He said that after failing to locate the corpses of his wife and children, he hid between two old fallen trees in the swamp. Meanwhile, the Indians pillaged everything they could find inside the McLane cabin before setting it afire.

The next morning, John and his stepfather, accompanied by a group of volunteers, left Pickett's cabin and returned to the scene of the massacre. After discovering the mutilated remains of John's mother and sisters, the volunteers set off in pursuit of the war party. After several hours, they called a halt to the search. None of the marauding Indians were ever captured.

A year later, Pascofa's Creeks signed a peace treaty with the whites. Through an interpreter, the chief said that the war would have continued if his son had not been shot and killed during a raid up on the Tallogee. At that moment, John McLane realized that his lucky shot had inadvertently brought an end to the Creek War. He kept the young chief's bow as a reminder of the tragic occurrences of that fateful day.

All traces of the McLane cabin are long gone. The site of the massacre is located deep in the woods on private property not far from Greensboro. A concrete monument erected in the twentieth century serves as a memorial to the victims. Not surprisingly, this lonely spot is said to be haunted by the ghosts of the McLane family. In the early 2000s, a group of paranormal investigators—the Big Bend Ghost Trackers—conducted a formal investigation of the site. During most of the night, the team members felt as if they were being watched. Midway through the investigation, one of the sensitive members began communicating with the spirit of a little girl standing near a tree. At the same time, another team member took a photograph of the tree. In the resulting photograph, the distinct images of a small orb by the tree and a larger orb a few feet away are visible. Another large orb was photographed hovering over the members while they congregated around the concrete memorial.

5
MARIANNA

THE RUSS HOUSE

Joseph Russ, a well-to-do merchant, built the Russ House at 4318 West Lafayette for himself and his mother, Mary Beman Russ. The mansion stands on the site of Battle of Marianna, where the Union Second Maine Cavalry encountered heavy resistance from Confederate troops on September 27, 1864. After Russ's mother died in 1897, he married Bettie Erwin Phillips in 1899. Bettie gave birth to their only child, Frances Phillips Russ, in 1900. In 1910, he converted the Queen Anne Victorian home into the Classical Revival style by adding columns. He also created a two-story round tower, on top of which was a cupola. Ten years later, the upper porch was transformed into a nursery for Frances's first child. The mercantile business that Joseph ran with Alexander Merritt was highly successful. Three months later, the couple's wedded bliss came to an abrupt end when Joseph lost his money in the Stock Market Crash of 1920. Bettie died in 1925; four months later, Joseph married Wilma "Willie" Treadwell. In 1930, three months after his wedding, Joseph shot himself in front of the mantle in his bedroom. Joseph's young widow and Frances each received half of the estate. Most of the land surrounding the mansion was sold off to pay a lien that the City of Mariana had placed against the property. Frances mortgaged the house to buy her stepmother's share of the home. After Frances's marriage to a former baseball player ended in divorce in 1937, she had to mortgage the home once again to pay for her children's college educations. In 1982, the Russ House, which was beginning to show its age, was placed on the National Register of Historic Places. After Frances died in 1989, her granddaughter Merrit Dekle was asked to donate the house to the county. The family donated the Russ House to Jackson County in 1995. The mansion was extensively restored between 1996 and 2000. It is now the county's visitor center and the home of the Jackson County Chamber of Commerce.

A house where five generations of the same family lived is bound, according to parapsychologists, to contain memories, some of which take the form of spirits. The apparition of a man with a moustache has been sighted at the top of the stairs. The same figure was photographed standing inside one of the tower windows that serves as a skylight for the second floor. Not surprisingly, the most haunted house in Marianna has attracted a number of different groups of paranormal investigators. One such group documented the mysterious opening and closing of the elevator door. The members also detected the whiff of perfume inside the house. On March 3, 2012, a group called Emerald Coast Paranormal Concepts conducted an all-night investigation of the old house. One of the members was drawn to a large meeting room, where the group conducted an EVP (electronic voice phenomena) session using digital recorders inside the room and captured a couple startling spectral voices that no one had heard before the recording was played back. The members also filmed one of the doors in the upper bathroom opening and closing on its own. One of their video cameras also recorded the lights blinking on and off, as well as the sound of footsteps. Three members of the group clearly heard a voice screaming "Help!" The group suspected that some of the paranormal activity encountered that night could have been generated by the soldiers who died in the Battle of Marianna.

So many ghost stories have been told about the Russ House over the years that one of the former residents warned the employees of the Chamber of Commerce not to stay in the mansion after dark. This old family mansion, the unique architecture of which has made it emblematic of the entire city of Marianna, is also rapidly gaining notoriety for its ghostly inhabitants.

BELLAMY BRIDGE

Bellamy Bridge stretches across the Chipola River half a mile north of Mariana. It can be reached by taking Bellamy Heritage Trail on Highway 162. Because the old iron bridge is in such an isolated location, it would probably be totally forgotten were in not for the legend of the ghost of Elizabeth Bellamy.

The legend of the ghost of Bellamy Bridge has been told and re-told so many times over the past 150 years that a number of variants have been produced. The basic plot of the story focuses on two of Marianna's earliest settlers, Dr. Samuel C. Bellamy and his wife, Elizabeth Jane Croom Bellamy. The date of their wedding is given as 1835, 1836 and 1837, but all versions of the tale agree that the wedding was held in the beautiful home that Dr. Bellamy had built especially for his bride. Most versions of the tale have it that she was dancing with her husband when suddenly her wedding gown brushed against a lighted candelabra and caught fire. Others say that she was dancing too close to the fireplace, and her dress was ignited by the open flames. In still another version of the tale, Elizabeth was seated in a chair, taking a break from all the dancing, when she accidentally knocked a candle off the table onto her dress. In all the variants, Elizabeth runs screaming out of the house into the night. Samuel and his brother, Edward, caught up with her after she collapsed and fell in a smoldering heap to the ground. They wrapped her up in a rug and carried her inside the house to one of the bedrooms. Just before she died a few days later in terrible agony, Elizabeth, with her last breath, told her husband, "I will love you forever." Dr. Bellamy never fully recovered from the loss of his beloved wife. He soon became a hopeless alcoholic and killed himself by slashing his throat with a razor in 1853 while on a visit to Chattahoochee.

The discrepancies in the various versions of the legend might lead one to view the story with a skeptical eye. The fact is, though, that Elizabeth and Samuel Bellamy really lived. In his book *The Ghost of Bellamy Bridge: 10 Ghosts and Monsters from Jackson County, Florida*, author Dale Cox says that Elizabeth Jane Croom and Samuel Bellamy were born into prominent families in North Carolina. The couple was married in North Carolina on July 15, 1837. At the time, Elizabeth was in her late teens, and Samuel was nine years older. They moved to Rock Cave Plantation, just northwest of Marianna. The bottomlands were ideal for growing cotton, but Samuel's prosperity came at a heavy price. The plantation's close proximity to the Chipola River made it vulnerable to infestations of mosquitoes. Elizabeth and her eighteen-month-old son, Alexander, contracted malaria. She passed away on May 11, 1837; Alexander died seven days later. They were buried in the family cemetery on a plantation owned by Samuel's brother, Edward, near the Chipola River. Although Samuel was heartbroken from the loss of his wife and child, he was able to pull his life together, at least for a while. He began working at the Union Bank and became a delegate to the 1838 Florida Constitutional Convention. He took out a sizable loan from the Union Bank to finance the construction of a large plantation house, but when the Union Bank collapsed, Samuel was ruined. He became severely depressed and began drinking heavily. Judging that his brother was incapable of running the plantation, Edward seized control of Samuel's property. Samuel sued Edward in an attempt to regain possession of his property, but he slit his own throat in 1853 before the case was settled.

No one knows for certain why Elizabeth Bellamy's ghost is said to haunt the Bellamy Bridge, which was erected in 1914, decades after she died. Some people say that Elizabeth's spirit feels a strong connection to the site of the bridge because it was at this particular spot where Samuel asked for her hand in marriage. Others say that she roams this area because she is buried nearby. The most plausible explanation for Elizabeth Bellamy's reappearance is the possibility that this historical figure has been melded in the legends with a fictional character in a novel by nineteenth-century novelist Caroline Lee Hertz, who lived in Mariana. In her novel *Ernest Linwood of the Long Moss Spring*, she described the tragic death of a young bride whose dress caught fire during a dance at Bellamy Plantation. Regardless of the reason Elizabeth's spirit haunts the bridge, the fact remains the many people claim to have seen her ghost here. Witnesses have seen the transparent form of a woman wearing a white dress walking down the dirt road leading to the bridge. A woman in white has also been sighted emerging from her grave and creeping through the woods lining the river. Others say that a "burning woman" runs up to the bridge with flames trailing behind her and then jumps into the river. According to another legend, Elizabeth has been known to take the form of a flaming ball of fire that plummets into the river. One can only wonder about the other forms Elizabeth will take as she continues to wander through the swamp, looking for her husband, who really did "lose his way" after her death.

6
MONTICELLO

EAST DOGWOOD STREET

Monticello, Florida, has the reputation of being a very haunted town. The PBS television network went so far as to call Monticello "The South's Most Haunted Small Town," and ABC-TV News deemed Monticello "The Most Haunted Small Town in America." Indeed, this small town does seem to have more than its share of haunted places, such as the Palmer House, the 1872 John Denham House Bed and Breakfast and the Monticello Opera House. Not surprisingly, ghost tours and cemetery tours attract thousands of visitors to Monticello every year. A number of theories have been proposed for the town's high concentration of paranormal activity, the most fascinating of which has to do with a phenomenon called ley-lines.

Ley-lines are the geometric alignments of natural and man-made sites, such as mounds, standing stones, water markers, churches, crossroads, hill forts and notches in hills. The theory that the lines connecting these places are imbued with some type of spiritual energy can be traced to the ancient Chinese art of *feng shui*. Practitioners in this field arranged buildings, stones and planted trees to conform to the "dragon currents" flowing along these lines. The routes taken by funeral parties in Europe and America for centuries are believed by some to be "spirit paths" for the movement of the souls. The theory of spirit lines did not receive prominence until the summer of 1921 when a successful beer salesman and self-taught archaeologist named Alfred Watkins was riding through Herefordshire, England, when he had an epiphany. Watkins began

People walking down East Dogwood Street have experienced sudden drops in temperature.

taking notice of a network of lines linking ancient sites and holy places. In 1925 at age seventy, Watkins published *The Old Straight Track*. In this book, Watkins theorized that ancient travelers followed a series of geographical markers following roads he called "ley-lines" because the word "ley" appears in many ancient place names. Monoliths such as "sighting posts" and "mark stones" were set up to mark these ancient trade routes. Watkins's Michell's Ley follows the path of the sun on May 8 and passes through a number of megalithic sites, the most noteworthy of which is Stonehenge. In combining Watkins's theory with the concept of *feng shui*, Michell revived the old belief that ley-lines are imbued with some sort of mystical power.

Today, many people dismiss ley-lines as being nothing more than an invention of New Age occultists. However, for many years, people walking down East Dogwood Street in Monticello have reported experiencing sensations that are commonly attributed to ley-lines, such as a dramatic drop in temperature on days when the air is completely still. Occasionally, a man wearing a grey uniform is sighted strolling down East Dogwood. This writer personally experienced being overcome by a wave of coldness while walking down the street in October 2012. Perhaps East Dogwood Street is a type of funerary path on which the spirits of the dead tread for eternity.

MONTICELLO OPERA HOUSE

Haunted theaters have been part of the paranormal landscape in the American South almost since the country's inception. Most of these theaters, such as Le Petite Theatre in New Orleans, are haunted by people who worked there, like stagehands and actors and actresses. The Monticello Opera House is unique in that it seems to be haunted by the man who built it.

John H. Perkins was a nineteenth-century businessman who made a fortune in his mercantile and cotton trading enterprises. In the late 1880s, he decided to capitalize on the large number of northerners who were taking Henry Plant's railroad to spend the winter in southern destinations. In 1890, he erected the Monticello Opera House at 185 West Washington Street. This beautiful Romanesque Revival building housed a general store, a farm implement supply store, a sewing machine shop and a general store. The opera house and foyer took up the entire second floor. It soon achieved fame for its unparalleled acoustics and its huge stage, which was the largest in the entire area. Livestock was sold from a stable behind the opera house,

The success of the Monticello Opera House was short-lived, however. In the early 1900s, the railroad was rerouted around Monticello, primarily

The ghost of John H. Perkins, who built the "Perkins Corner" in 1890, is said to haunt the opera house.

because a disagreement between the locals and the owners of the railroad. Not long after the railroad tracks were pulled up, the Monticello Opera House closed because the wealthy patrons who had been taking the train to Monticello were now wintering in places south of Thomasville. For decades, the Monticello Opera House stood empty. By the late 1960s, it was showing the effects of neglect and the passing of time. In 1972, the Monticello Opera House was on the verge of being demolished when a group of interested citizens came to its aid. They formed the Monticello Opera Company in March 1972 and began raising funds to renovate the historic building. Contributions from local residents, most notably Mrs. Dorothy Simpson, and a grant from the State of Florida enabled the organization to buy the Perkins Block on October 17, 1973. The building's original architectural features, such as candy-colored stained glass, were preserved with the exception of the seats on the main level of the theater, which had to be replaced. A few modern improvements have been made in the old building as well. An elevator was installed in 1999; in 2004, the Monticello Opera House became accessible for people with disabilities.

Today, the old opera house serves Monticello as an all-purpose community center. Weddings and receptions are held on the patio and in the gazebo out back. Children's theater performances, large musicals and murder mystery dinners are also part of the opera house's offerings. People attending these events claim that the ghost of John H. Perkins makes an occasional appearance as well. His apparition has been seen many times peeking through the curtains. The ghostly image of a distinguished-looking man has also been captured in the balcony. The faint tones of piano music have been heard throughout the opera house. During an investigation conducted by the Big Bend Ghost Trackers, members watching the monitor observed a brilliant orb floating around another member who was dancing on the stage in time to a waltz that was being played. Mr. Perkins's ghostly presence inside the Monticello Opera House suggests that he approves of the community's efforts to restore the old building to its former glory.

THE JOHN DENHAM HOUSE BED AND BREAKFAST

John Denham was an immigrant from Dunbar, Scotland, who made most of his fortune as a cotton merchant, although he did make a good living during the Civil War providing supplies to the Confederate army. In 1872, he built

Local merchant John Denham built this mansion in 1872.

his two-story Italianate mansion near the center of Monticello. The mansion was noteworthy because it was crowned with a cupola. In the nineteenth century, houses built along the seacoast had cupolas so that the wives of sea captains could gaze out at the ocean in search of their husbands. Denham climbed up into his cupola so that he could watch his workers laboring in the fields and spy on his neighbors.

Following John Denham's death in 1874, a succession of new owners moved into the showplace of Monticello. The second owner of the house was Virginia C. Turnbull (1869–1939). Mrs. O. Lacy was the third owner; three generations of her family lived in John Denham's former home. For short periods of time, the house stood empty between owners. The current owner, Patricia Inmon, converted the mansion into a bed-and-breakfast. The John Denham House was listed on the National Register of Historic Places in 1982.

Rumors of the ghosts inside the John Denham House began in those short periods when the house stood empty. People walking by the house claimed to have heard people talking and music being played behind closed doors. Reports of ghostly activity escalated soon after the John Denham House became a bed-and-breakfast. The innkeeper said that on several occasions each month, the alarm clocks in the guest rooms started ringing at the same time. Guest experienced cold spots in specific parts of the house. An unseen hand was said to turn lights on and off in the guest rooms. Many guests who had just put new batteries in their digital cameras have told Patricia Inmon that their cameras were drained of energy while they were standing inside the cupola. The first owner of the house—John Denham—may have made an occasional appearance in the house. Guests have seen the ghostly figure of a man wearing nineteenth-century clothing standing in the hallway outside the guest rooms on the second floor. One guest reported seeing this same man inside one of the guest rooms. The apparition of a Union soldier has also been seen on the grounds of the mansion.

The most haunted room in the John Denham House Bed and Breakfast is the Blue Room. This particular guest room is said to be haunted by the spirit of a lonely woman known only as "Aunt Sarah," whom Pat Inmon describes as "the old maid sister of Dr. Williams. She never got married, and she never had children. She died there in 1910, and she comes back to haunt the Blue Room." In their book *The Florida Guide to Haunted Locations*, authors Chad Lewis and Terry Fisk write that Aunt Sarah had wanted to get married and have children, but for some unknown reason, her marriage never took place. Pat Inmon said not long after she bought the old house, a mother with several children told her that the light suddenly turned itself on in the middle of the night while she was staying in the Blue Room. Pat's daughter had a disturbing experience inside the Blue Room not long after her baby was born: "My daughter tells that story that the baby never slept all night in that room. My daughter is skeptical [of the ghost stories], but she swears that Aunt Sarah was patting her baby during the night." Other guests with small children have reported being tucked into bed by phantom hands in the Blue Room. Some people believe that Aunt Sarah disturbs mothers and their babies in the Blue Room because she never had any children of her own and is jealous.

Another legend about Aunt Sara's ghost appeared in *Haunted Monticello, Florida*, by Betty Davis and the Big Bend Ghost Trackers. For years, people spread the rumor that Aunt Sarah had regularly rendezvoused with a married politician in the Blue Room while most of the ladies in town were attending temperance meetings on Wednesdays. The illicit lovers are said to have made their presence known in a variety of different ways. The television has been known to turn itself on and off. Guests have seen a rocking chair in the Blue Room rock all by itself.

Pat Inmon has become a believer in the ghosts occupying the Blue Room, primarily because of the consistency of the stories she hears from guests. "You'd hear a story about the Blue Room at breakfast, and then two weeks later, you'd hear the same story. Then maybe six months later, you'd hear the same story again. There is definitely some kind of presence in that room. I have also heard several stories from guests about experiencing a cold sensation upstairs."

Another haunted room in the John Denham House Bed and Breakfast is the Gold Room. "One night, a couple spent the night in the Gold Room, and they were spooked to death," Pat Inmon said. "The man and women said that the chairs were rocking and the baby's car seat was moving back and forth by itself."

One of the bed-and breakfast's least publicized ghosts is the spirit of a little dog. "My ex-husband always let him get up and sleep on the bed next to him," Pat said. "I didn't like having the dog sleep in our bed, but he let him do it anyway. After my husband left, the dog died. Later, I'd hear the patter of dog feet in the house. I checked outside, and all the dogs were asleep. I got up and saw the imprint of where the dog had slept in the bed."

People also claim to see spirits inside the cupola. One such manifestation occurred when this writer was taking a ghost tour hosted by the Big Bend Ghost Trackers on October 18, 2012. My wife, Marilyn, and I had booked a room in the John Denham House for the night. The tour guide was telling the story of Aunt Sarah when a man on the tour observed a female figure sitting inside the cupola. Within a few seconds, several other fingers began pointing up to the cupola. In the interests of paranormal investigation, I felt obligated to inform the ghost enthusiasts that my wife had told me before the tour that she was going to read a book inside the cupola some time during the evening. The tour guide added that debunking ghost sightings is as essential to ghost hunting as proving that they actually exist.

The John Denham House Bed and Breakfast is such an active location that the Big Bend Ghost Trackers offer ghost tracking seminars inside the old house on a regular basis. "During one of the seminars they hold here," Pat said, "they were doing meditations to summon the spirits. Finally, Betty said [to the medium], 'Call 'em out.' And that did it! Ghosts popped all over the place. Betty doesn't fabricate evidence. Her photographs and readings are authentic."

Pat Inmon admits, though, that spending the night in her bed-and-breakfast can be a terrifying experience for some people: "Two people got so scared that they just walked out the door. One lady was frightened from

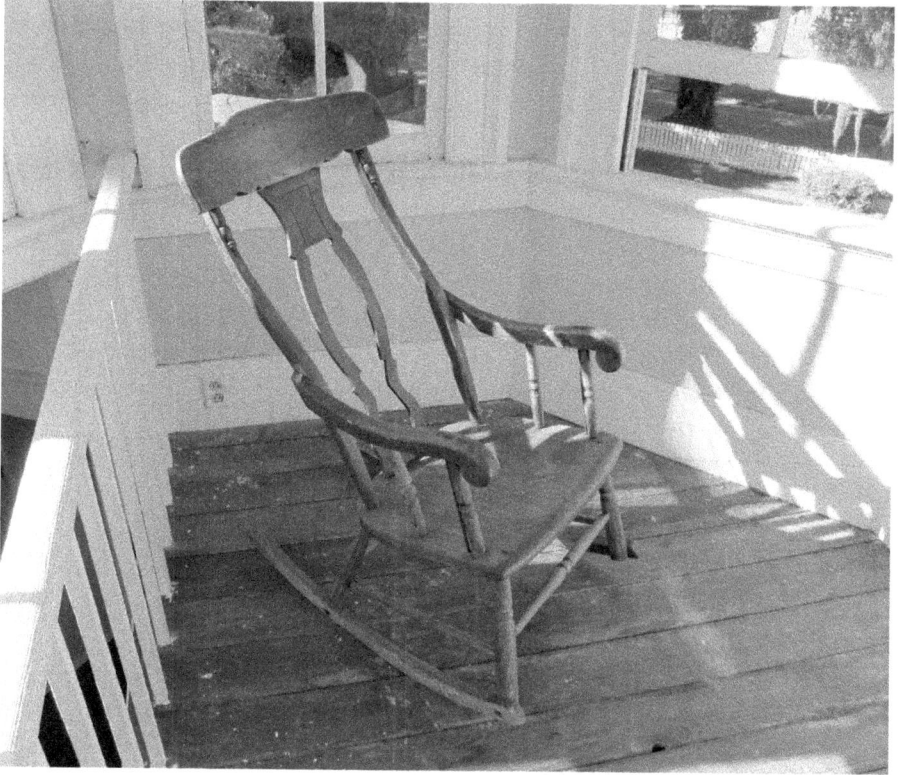

A ghostly figure is said to appear in the cupola of the John Denham House Bed and Breakfast.

the time she hit the front door. I mean, even before she got her own room key. Another guy just got up and left. He didn't even say, 'Goodbye.' He just dropped the key on the nightstand and left."

Any initial reservations Pat might have had about living and working in a haunted house soon gave way to curiosity: "When you look through a microscope, you can see the unseen world. That's how it is for me with a digital camera. I am seeing the unseen world."

THE AVERA–CLARKE HOUSE

A Civil War veteran named Judge Thomas Clarke built the Avera-Clarke House in 1890. He attended law school in Georgia after the war. In the late 1800s, Clarke moved to Monticello to practice law. Two of the high points of the judge's illustrious career include signing the Second Florida Constitution and founding the Farmers and Merchants Bank. He lived in the house with his wife and four children until he died suddenly in 1900. His son, Judge S.D. Clarke, was the last member of the Clarke family who owned and lived in the house. In 2003, Gretchen and Troy Avera purchased the historic home with the purpose of converting it into a bed-and-breakfast. During the restoration, the couple made a concerted effort to preserve the historical ambience of the home. The alleged presence of the ghost of at least one of the former occupants suggests that Gretchen and Troy might have succeeded more than they realized.

Ghostly activity has been reported in several places in the Avera-Clarke House. A number of guests have photographed orbs in front of the fireplace in the dining room. Not surprisingly, this is also the place where Judge Thomas Clarke's wake was held. Orbs have also appeared in photographs taken on the staircase leading to the second floor.

A ghost is also said to inhabit another structure on the property: the Cottage. Originally known as the "Greenhouse," the Cottage was built in 1821 and moved from its original location near the courthouse in 2006, just before it was scheduled to be razed. This historic building is said to be haunted by the ghost of a woman. Shortly after the house was moved, a guest staying at the Avera-Clarke House claimed to have seen the specter of a woman on the porch of the Cottage. Orbs have been captured just outside of the Cottage.

The Avera-Clarke House promotes itself as the perfect location for receptions of all sorts, including club meetings, birthdays, weddings and baby showers. The covered veranda, which seats 150 people, is the ideal venue for special events. One cannot rule out the possibility, however, that some of the people who absorb the southern charm of the Avera-Clarke are of the ghostly variety.

The Meeting Oak

Standing just a few feet away from the Jefferson County Courthouse is a majestic oak tree known locally as "The Meeting Oak." According to a historic marker that has been placed next to the 250-year-old tree, it received its name because Confederate soldiers met here before being assigned to their respective units. One can only imagine the emotional

The Meeting Oak derives its name from the Confederate soldiers who gathered here before being mustered out.

outpouring that characterized these gatherings as the young men said their tearful goodbyes to their families and their sweethearts. Legend has it that one of these soldiers had such a strong personal connection to this place that his spirit can still be seen standing at attention with his shiny new musket.

According to another local legend, prisoners were hanged from the old tree on Thursday afternoons after they had been sentenced to death in the adjacent courthouse. People say that some businesses in Monticello still close after 12:00 p.m. as a continuation of this tradition. However, Derylene Counts, a local historian who was interviewed by WCTV in 2010, had a different explanation for the Thursday afternoons: "Twenty-four merchants signed the petition to close the businesses because they wanted to practice and drill with the home guard. Now, this was getting ready for America's entrance into World War I, and they wanted to be a part of the drill in Monticello, and they closed their businesses on Thursday afternoon so that they could drill." The reporter also interviewed representatives for Monticello Milling and the U.S. Post Office, who said that they did not know how the tradition of closing on Thursday afternoons originated but that they still follow the practice because that is always the way it has been done. Indeed, turning one's back on customs that have been passed down for generations can be a very difficult change to make.

OLD JEFFERSON COUNTY JAIL

The Old Jefferson County Jail on the corner of Dogwood and Water Streets is one of the few century-old jails that look much the same as they did in the early years because the steel has not been removed. It was constructed soon after the first jail on Mulberry Street burned down in 1906, probably around 1908. The jail is unique in that the sheriff and his family lived on the first floor and the prisoners occupied the second floor. The basement was used for storage. As was typical of the time period, the prisoners were segregated. Whites were housed in the two cells in the front part of the jail; blacks lived in the rear part. The sheriff's three-bedroom apartment had a dining room, a living room and a kitchen. A steel door just beyond the staircase separated the sheriff's family's apartment from the sheriff's office and the stairway leading to the jail. The small building in the back was the women's jail. Most of the female prisoners assisted the sheriff's wife with preparing meals for the prisoners. The prisoners were served meals in the morning and the afternoon. Breakfast was usually the same every day: grits, eggs, a biscuit and coffee. The sheriff's children slid the trays through slots in the cells. Some of the interior walls of the jail are covered with graffiti consisting mostly of calendars and prayers, such as "Lord help Harold Monk" and "Please help me."

The Old Jefferson County Jail closed in 1970. For many years, the Jefferson County Commission leased a large portion of the jail. At the time of this printing, a group of citizens called Main Street of Monticello, Florida, was attempting to raise funds to renovate the old building and turn it into a museum. Part of the group's plan is to restore the first floor to its 1930s appearance.

The organization's hope that the Jail Museum will become a destination point for tourists is bolstered by the stories that the historic structure is haunted, possibly by the spirit of a prisoner who died when he tried to break out. Ever since the jail closed, people walking past the building have reported hearing strange noises, such as eerie moans and the rattling of cell

Built around 1908, the Old Jefferson County Jail is said to be a hotbed of residual ghostly activity.

The moans of prisoners held in small, cramped cells like this one can still be heard in the Old Jefferson County Jail.

doors. Visitors standing inside the cells have captured orbs on their cameras. In her book *Haunted Monticello, Florida,* author Betty Davis suggests that the ghost haunting the old jail is the spirit of Sheriff Thompson Brooks Simkins, who was shot and killed on December 29, 1899, by Will Gorman. Many people have seen the vigilant figure of an armed man dressed in a turn-of-the-century suit, walking around the jail at night. For some dedicated souls, duty is a calling that transcends the passing of time and even life itself.

JEFFERSON COUNTY HIGH SCHOOL

Jefferson County High School at 425 West Washington Street was designed by architect Samuel Carroll. Built in the Greek Revival style with slave labor in 1852, it was Florida's first brick school building. The bricks were fired on the George Taylor Plantation. In the early years, the school was known as the Jefferson Academy. The building originally housed the primary public school; in 1889, it became the primary high school. According to Betty Davis, author of *Haunted Monticello, Florida,* all of the teachers were male in the early years. During the Civil War, two female teachers—Elizabeth McCants and Ella Rhodes—were hired to teach in the academy. After the Civil War, a Confederate veteran named Colonel William O. Girdeau was appointed headmaster of the academy. Two major structural changes were made in 1915. Corinthian columns were added to the main entrance, and the building was expanded on the east and west sides.

By the end of the twentieth century, the Jefferson County High School had been replaced by more modern buildings. In the years that the old school has stood empty, many people have reported evidence of paranormal activity inside the historic structure. Guests staying in the John Denham House Bed and Breakfast across the street claim to have seen a blue light at the top of the building. At the time of this writing, the Jefferson County High School was being renovated for use as a civic center. Members of the construction crews who have worked on the site are convinced that the old Jefferson County High School is haunted. Some of the workmen who have spent the night in trailers have heard the musical laughter of children from inside the building. The most frequently reported ghostly sound is a strange rap-tap-tap noise that has been heard by workmen and recorded by ghost hunting groups. The sound is said to resemble the tapping of a wooden ruler on a desk. Many people who have taken the Big Bend Ghost Trackers' ghost

Jefferson County High School is the first brick school in the state of Florida.

tours have captured orbs inside the school by placing their cameras directly on the window to avoid reflection. I took several photographs inside one of the rooms after dark and captured an orb in only one of the pictures. The skeptic in me ascribes the strange disks of light to bugs or dust. However, like many people who visit the Jefferson County High School, I like to think that the orb is the spiritual energy from a ghostly teacher who is still trying to keep order in the classroom. As any educator will testify, this is a never-ending task.

THE DAFFODALE HOUSE

The imposing Victorian-era mansion at 620 West Washington Street was built between 1897 and 1904. The first owner is said to have been a rich banker and politician who had wanted a house befitting his position in the community. Down through the years, the house has been embellished by its subsequent owners. Since 2006, it has been run as a bed-and-breakfast by Cathy and Scotty Ebberbach, who are proud of their home's connection

The Safari Room in the Daffodale House is said to be haunted by the ghost of a woman in white.

to the past. The couple proudly displays the pocket doors, the butler bells and the 1927 elevator. They even give ghost tours to people interested in exploring the house's ghostly mysteries.

The Ebberbachs sensed that they were sharing their beautiful home with an otherworldly guest not long after they began renovations. After Scott photographed the new tiles that he and his son had laid in the back hallway, he was surprised to find that he had captured the image of a white figure. The Ebberbach family soon discovered that the distinctive odor of cigar smoke seemed to hover around the elevator. The lights in the front room turned themselves back on after they were turned off. In her book *Hauntings in Florida's Panhandle*, author Nicole Carlson Easley said that one of the couple's sons had a terrifying experience while he was asleep in the Safari Room. At 3:00 a.m., he opened his eyes and was startled by what he saw. A woman in a white dress was standing in front of the door. Her lips were moving, as if she was in the middle of a conversation with someone who was not there. The boy was so frightened that he dashed out of the Safari Room and ran into his parents' bedroom.

Much of the paranormal activity in the house seems to center around the attic. On many occasions, the innkeepers have heard someone walking around up there. Hearing footsteps in the attic is particularly disturbing considering that not only is the attic used purely for storage, but the door is securely locked as well. The possibility exists that the spirits of people who used to live in the attic are still making their presence known. During an investigation conducted by the Big Bend Ghost Hunters, a motion detector that had been set up in the attic went off twice during the night. None of the investigators were up in the attic at the time.

Cathy and Scotty Ebberbach have definitely learned to live with their ghosts, whom they consider to be benign. Like most people who live in a haunted house, they have grown to expect to hear strange sounds now and then or to encounter the unexplained in dark corners. Many of their guests are people who, like them, are intrigued by the possibility that ghosts walk among us.

THE PALMER HOUSE

The Palmer House, just down the street from the courthouse, looks like hundreds of other Greek Revival antebellum homes. Surprisingly, this homey-looking white frame house is one of the most haunted buildings in Monticello. It was built at the corner of Palmer Mill Road and South Jefferson Street in 1840 by Dr. Thomas Martin Palmer, who was surgeon general of the Confederacy. His son, Dr. Dabney Palmer, inherited the home. Dr. Palmer seemed to be just another well-respected small town doctor. He lived in his father's house with his mother; his wife, Laura Willie; their small son; and a young African American woman named Lilla Prince. However, a close examination of Dr. Palmer's personal life reveals that he was anything but a run-of-the-mill physician.

Dr. Palmer's professional interests extended beyond general practice. He wrote several books on medicine and chemistry, and during much of his career, Dabney Palmer served in the roles of pharmacist and undertaker, in addition to his duties as doctor. The small building outside of his private home served as his office. The basement of his home served as the mortuary. Legend has it that Dr. Palmer believed that the blood should be removed from the body and buried with the corpse. He was assisted by a black man nicknamed "Poltergeist" because he was rumored to cast no shadow. After the grave was dug and the body was interred, Poltergeist poured the bucket full of blood into the grave.

In 1880, the Palmer House was sold to John H. Perkins, who built the Monticello Opera House and other buildings on what has become known as "The Perkins Block." Over the years, a number of different families have lived in the historic home. In recent years, it has housed an antique store. By the time Jackie Anders bought and restored the old house, it was already known as a haunted house.

One of the ghostly legends concerns what folklorists call "the ineradicable bloodstain." In her book *Haunted Monticello, Florida,* author Betty Davis says that Dr. Palmer got into an argument inside the house with Poltergeist, who threw a bucket of blood on him. Some of the blood splashed against the wall. For many years, the bloodstain resisted all efforts to remove it, including applying numerous coats of paint and scrubbing it with household cleaners. The story goes that removing the wall seemed to be the only way to permanently remove the blood. When one of the owners removed a picture hanging on the wall in the room below the room with the bloodstained wall, she was shocked to find what appeared to be a faded crimson stain.

This small structure outside of the Palmer House was used by Dr. Palmer as an office.

This statue outside of the Palmer House is said to turn when visitors pass by.

Betty Davis reports that Dr. Palmer has left his mark on the property in another way as well. The figure of a man dressed in a nineteenth-century suit has been sighted walking briskly from the office to the house. Even in death, Dr. Palmer is still keeping his busy schedule.

In her book *Hauntings in Florida's Panhandle*, author Nicole Carlson Easley says that the Anders family has had a number of unsettling experiences inside the Palmer House. Spectral footsteps have been heard descending the staircase. Some customers say that they have heard a ghostly female voice inside the store. The most frightening ghostly occurrence inside the house is a cool breeze that wafts through part of the house. Shortly after Jackie Anders was given the house as a birthday present from her husband, she was packing items in a box when she experienced coldness sweep across her body. Not long thereafter, her daughter was alone in the pink room when she felt a puff of cold air in her ear.

Today, the Palmer House is a regular stop on ghost tours conducted by the Big Bend Ghost Trackers. Some people on the tour have photographed the image of a little girl standing in front of one of the windows in the front of the building. A statue sitting on the side of the house is said to change directions from one day to the next.

The Palmer House was added to the U.S. Register of Historic Places on November 21, 1978. Not surprisingly, this historically haunted house is at the top of the list of places to investigate for most of the paranormal groups in the state of Florida.

7
PORT ST. JOE

THE GULF COUNTY COURTHOUSE

The history of Port St. Joe is very closely connected to that of the old town of St. Joseph, which became the largest city in the Territory of Florida only two years after its founding on the shores of St. Joseph Bay. Because over six thousand people lived in St. Joseph, it was chosen as the site of the first Constitutional Convention for Florida. The Convention assembled on December 3, 1838, and lasted for thirty-four days. The delegates completed a draft of the first of Florida's five constitutions on January 11, 1839. This document served as the cornerstone of Florida's government until the Civil War. The city of St. Joseph, however, did not last nearly as long as the constitution that was drafted there. A yellow fever epidemic, which was said to have been brought to St. Joseph by a ship in 1841, decimated the city. In 1843, the abandoned buildings were completely obliterated by a massive hurricane. The present city of Port St. Joe was established two miles north of St. Joseph. Port St. Joe retains the cemetery where the yellow fever victims are interred, as well as St. Joseph's name and its nickname—"The Constitutional City."

The Gulf County Courthouse was erected shortly after Port St. Joe became the county seat in 1964. It was generally regarded as nothing more than a functional government building until July 28, 1987. Sixty-two-year-old Clyde Melvin had been divorced eight months when he entered the judge's chambers. Unhappy about the alimony payments he was ordered to pay, Melvin shot and killed his sister-in-law, Circuit Judge Wilson Lamar Bradley and a divorce lawyer. Melvin's ex-wife was wounded. Afterward, Clyde Melvin was ordered to serve four life sentences.

The aftermath of these senseless shootings led to stronger security measures inside the courthouse and to reports of strange occurrences. Weird flashing lights began appearing in the judge's chambers where the shootings began. Employees reported elevators moving between floors when no one was inside. A number of witnesses claim to have heard someone running on the catwalk connecting the courtroom and the jail.

Port St. Joe has tried to move past the tragic events of July 28, 1987. It is focusing most of its energies in making the transition from an industrial city to becoming a tourist destination. In light of the general public's current fascination with the paranormal, one wonders if the ghostly activity inside the courthouse will ever be promoted as part of the city's allure.

8
QUINCY

THE ALLISON HOUSE

Abraham Kirkendolle Allison, the original owner of the Allison House, was one of Quincy's most prominent citizens. He was born December 10, 1810, in Jones County, Georgia. His parents were Captain James and Sarah Fannin Allison. After graduating from high school, Allison worked as a merchant, first in Columbus, Georgia, and then in Henry County, Alabama. After moving to Apalachicola, he became the city's first mayor in 1832. He was also elected the first county judge of Franklin County and clerk of the United States. He first achieved notoriety in the 1830s, when he served as a captain of the Franklin Rifles in the Seminole War and as a general in the Wars of Indian Removal. In 1839, Allison moved to Quincy; four years later, he built a home in the Georgian colonial style at the corner of King and Madison Streets. By the 1850s, Allison's political aspirations had broadened. He was elected Speaker of the Florida House in 1852. In the absence of Governor Thomas Brown and Senate President R.J. Floyd, both of whom were out of state, Allison became acting governor on September 16, 1835. He surrendered the office to James E. Broome on October 3. Allison was elected delegate to the Constitutional Convention of 1861 and served in the Florida State Senate between 1862 and 1864. When Governor John Milton committed suicide on April 1, 1865, Allison was serving as president of the state senate. He immediately assumed the duties of governor and served in the position until resigning the office on

The Allison House was built in 1843 for the sixth governor of Florida, A.K. Allison.

May 19, 1865. The day before Federal troops occupied Tallahassee, Allison went into hiding but was captured on June 19, 1865. He was incarcerated at Fort Pulaski for several months.

After the Civil War, Allison returned to Quincy and started a law practice. In 1867, Allison's wife, Elizabeth Susan Coleman, gave birth to a girl, Sarah, in their home. In 1870, Allison led a group of armed men to prevent African-Americans from voting in the election. He was indicted two years later on the charge of "intimidating Negroes." Allison was found guilty, fined and forced to serve six months in jail. He died in Quincy on July 8, 1893.

After his widow, Elizabeth, died in 1895, Sarah inherited the house. In 1925, she and her husband, Ross Gilliam Harris, had the family home moved to its present location at 215 North Madison Street. Workmen raised the house on brick pilings and added a second story; they also closed in the lower part of the house and created a boardinghouse on the upper floor. Sarah and Ross lived in what is now the Country Room downstairs. In the 1940s and 1950s, after the deaths of Sarah and Ross Harris, the upper floor of the house was converted into apartments. The space that is now the lobby became a credit bureau. In 1990, the old house received another makeover, this time as a bed-and-breakfast. Six years later, Stuart and Eileen Johnson bought the business.

The Johnsons began receiving reports of strange activity inside their bed-and-breakfast not long after purchasing it. One of these incidents occurred in the late 1990s. "My sister-in-law was staying in the Garden Room," Stuart said. "That night, she woke up and saw a woman in white sitting in a chair by her bed. The ghost told her everything was OK and to go back to sleep. The next night, she went to sleep in the same bed. Around midnight, she felt cold, so she woke up, intending to turn up the thermostat. This time, the woman in white was sitting on the end of the bed. She said, 'Don't be afraid. Go back to bed.'"

In 2002, her stories came to the attention of a local group of paranormal investigators called the Big Bend Ghost Trackers. They began setting up their equipment in two adjoining rooms—the Governor's Room and the Garden Room. One of the members, who is a sensitive, made contact with a young woman who identified herself as the governor's daughter, Sarah. The same team member also sensed that the governor's ghost was pacing up and

A member of a ghost hunting team saw ghost of a man pacing back and forth in the backyard of the Allison House.

down the hall in front of the Garden Room. "Later that night, they set up a video camera in front of the stairwell outside the Garden Room," Stuart said. "They caught the image of a ribbon of smoke floating up the stairs. A few seconds later, [the entity] moved around to the right side of the door to the Garden Room."

That same night, one of the ghost trackers saw a man pacing back and forth in the backyard. He looked up at the team member and said, "I'm looking for my wife." She replied, "She's gone to the hereafter. She's waiting for you there." Immediately, the man faded away.

Children seem to be especially sensitive to the spirits in the Allison House. In 2005, a woman, along with her two daughters and her nephew, checked into one of the upper rooms. That evening, her nine-year-old daughter sensed an uncanny presence in the room and began taking photographs with her digital camera. The next morning, when she and her family were checking out, the mother turned to the little girl and said, "Honey, do you want to show Mr. Johnson what you got?" The girl proceeded to show the photographs to Stuart Johnson. Every single picture that she took the night before had orbs.

The owners of the Allison House Inn are proud of the numerous rewards they have received, including Most Historic Inn, Best Breakfast in the Southeast and Most Affordable Luxury Bed & Breakfast. And, like many owners of haunted bed-and-breakfasts, they also embrace the inn's reputation as a haunted destination for ghost hunters.

THE LEAF THEATER

Built in 1949, the Leaf Theater derived its name from shade tobacco, one of the area's main cash crops at the time. For decades, the single-screen Leaf Theater, which could seat 1,200 people, was one of only two movie theaters in the area. Facing stiff competition with multiplex cinemas, television and video, the Leaf Theater was forced to close its doors in 1980. Three years later, the abandoned theater was purchased by a group of private citizens. With the assistance of grants and donations from private citizens, the Leaf Theater was restored. The stage was enlarged and now takes up over one-third of the original seating space. The Leaf Theater became the permanent home of a newly formed musical theater group, the Quincy Music Theater, which had been performing in churches and schools. The Quincy Music

The Quincy Music Theatre opened in 1949 as the Leaf Theater.

Theater's first production, *Lil' Abner*, was performed in the spring of 1984. Today, the Leaf Theater is regarded as more than a cinema treasure. It is, without a doubt, one of the most haunted buildings in town.

Ever since the Quincy Music Theater took up residence inside the Leaf Theater, a number of staff members have reported encounters with at least one ghostly entity inside the building. The doors had not been open for very long before employees began feeling uneasy in certain parts of the theater. Mysterious voices raised goose bumps on the arms of new staff members. Doors opened and slammed shut on their own. Disembodied footsteps resounded throughout the theater. Objects that were placed in one spot before the lights were turned off were found in an entirely different place the next day. Dark figures were spotted walking around the balcony. People working in the theater by themselves have felt a pair of invisible eyes staring at them.

Another one of the theater's spirits is the ghost of a little girl. She is usually sighted in the third row on the left side of the auditorium. In their book *The Florida Road Guide to Haunted Locations*, authors Chad Lewis and Terry Fisk tell the story of a former manager named Michael who was standing on a ladder while he was changing the stage light at 3:00 a.m. Suddenly, he saw a little girl standing in the third row, staring back up at him. Assuming that she had been accidentally locked inside the theater, he asked her what she was doing there. When she didn't answer, he descended the ladder. By the time he had walked over to the third row, she was gone.

The ghost of a "prim and proper" older woman also makes an occasional appearance inside the Leaf Theater. Witnesses say she is dressed in the fashions of the 1950s. According to Nicole Carlson Easley, author of *Hauntings in Florida's Panhandle*, she is the ghost of a woman who worked in the concession stand in the 1950s and 1960s. As a rule, she sat in the back of the right section of seats so that she could rush back to the lobby if someone wanted to buy something from the concession stand. She was sighted by an actor who was rehearsing his lines all by himself late one evening. Suddenly, he saw an older woman with her hair tied up in a bun, sitting in the back of the right section of seats.

The scariest part of the theater is the landing at the top of the stairs leading behind the auditorium to the old projection room. People walking

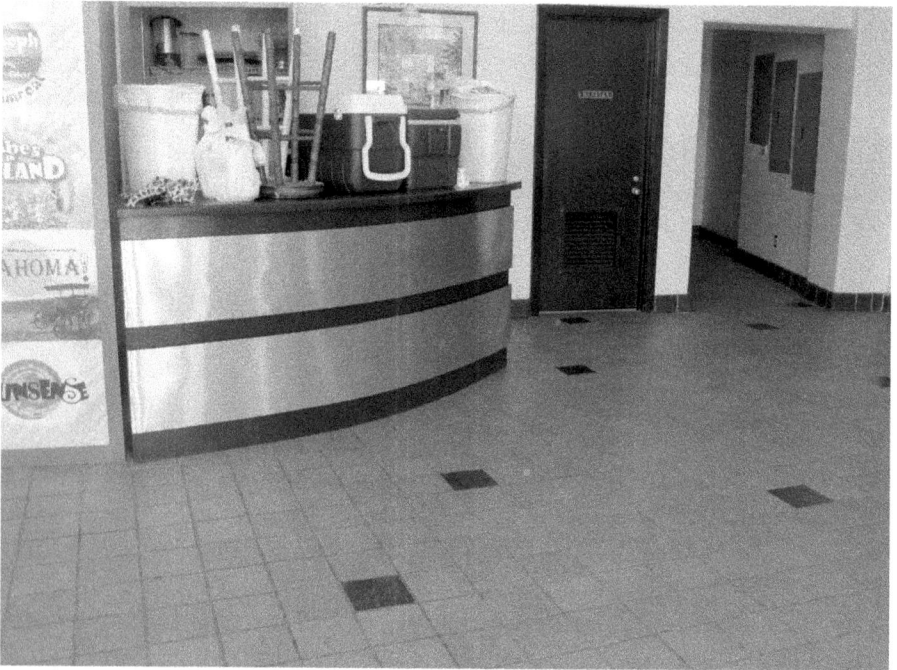

One of the ghosts haunting Leaf Theater is the spirit of a woman who worked in the concession stand in the 1950s and 1960s.

up the stairs to the landing have passed through what they describe as a "cold spot" that seems to be twenty degrees colder than the rest of the theater. A cleaning lady was vacuuming the landing one evening when she felt an invisible force fly right through her. She stopped vacuuming and ran down the stairs as fast as she could. Betty Davis, the executive director of the Big Bend Ghost Trackers, told author Nicole Carlson Easley that she saw the ghost of a man wearing a brown belt and khaki pants standing on the landing. He was tapping his watch and waving his arms, apparently in an effort to make her go away. Later on, Betty found out that this could be the ghost of the former projectionist.

The most commonly sighted apparition inside the Leaf Theater is the ghost of a short, stocky man wearing khaki pants. This spirit has been seen in the projection booth, the balcony and the auditorium itself. His favorite place to sit is in the third seat from the right end of the first row in the central section of seats. Longtime employees of the theater believe that he is the ghost of a projectionist named Sherille Odel McDaniel, who died in the late 1980s. Confirmation of the identity of this particular ghost was provided by the Big Bend Ghost Trackers. During an all-night investigation of the theater, one of the paranormal investigators made contact with a man she described as a short, stocky man wearing a brown belt and khaki pants. The next morning, the manager, Bill Mock, matched their description of the ghost with that of Mr. McDaniel, the former projectionist.

Bill Mock had his own ghostly episodes inside the theater. "Strange things happen, whether it's just a feeling, or…my name has been called out when I've been the only one here, and I turn around and nobody will be there and two minutes later, it's the same thing." Mock has also witnessed the strange behavior of one particular seat in the auditorium. Cleaning ladies have told him that the third seat from right in the front row of the central section refuses to stay folded up. One night, he decided to test the cleaning ladies' credibility by closing the seats himself. Sure enough, when he went back to check on the "ghost seat," it was unfolded.

In October 2012, the director of one of the theater's productions and the theater administrator had their own paranormal experience late one evening when they saw the figure of a man standing at the top of the steps leading to an outdoor storage room. Assuming that the man was a member of the stage crew who had not left with the others, the director yelled up to him, telling him that they were closing up for the night. When he got no response from the man, the administrator walked up the dark stairs. To his surprise, no one was there. Sensing that he and the director had just met a ghost, the administrator told the director about a death that occurred in the theater twenty years earlier. A middle-aged man was romancing a young woman inside the theater when he suffered a heart attack and died. The woman was not charged in the man's death because she had reported the incident to the police.

Today, the Quincy Music Theater is a fixture in the Quincy area. People travel from miles around to attend concerts featuring gospel singers, big band music, blues and opera singers and variety shows. The theater group has also tackled such large-scale productions as *Oklahoma* and *Fiddler on the Roof*. For some people, though, the most eagerly anticipated appearance at the former Leaf Theater is by one of the ghosts who are commemorated in a plaque presented by the Big Bend Ghost Hunters, certifying that the Leaf Theater is an actual haunted site.

9
SUMATRA

THE GHOST HEARSE OF SUMATRA

Sumatra is a small, unincorporated community in Liberty County, Florida. The original inhabitants of this region, the Apalachee Indians, left behind mounds and artifacts that date back to 1200 BC. Just south of Sumatra is Fort Gadsden. Built by the British during the War of 1812, the abandoned fort was taken over by 300 African American men and women, most of whom were runaway slaves, four years later. Twenty Choctaw warriors took refuge in the old fort as well. On July 27, 1816, the fort was surrounded by the Fourth U.S. Infantry and hundreds of Creek warriors. When the occupants refused to surrender, the gunboats opened fire. The fifth shot struck the gunpowder magazine and blew up the fort, killing 270 people.

One would think that Fort Gadsden would be the hub of Sumatra's ghostly activity. Although some visitors to the historic site have reported eerie feelings, no fully developed ghost stories have emerged from "the Negro Fort." Sumatra's best-known ghost story takes place at the railroad tracks. Legend has it that back in the 1960s, a hearse was transporting a body to Bloody Bluff Cemetery when it ran off the road and wrecked. Some say the driver was blinded by the high beams of an oncoming car. The driver was killed instantly. For many years, young people have spread the tale that if you park a car at the tracks, turn off the headlights and wait, a long black hearse will pull up behind you at 3:30 a.m. The ghostly driver will then follow you down Bloody Bluff Road, flashing his brights the entire way, apparently in an effort to make you run off the road. The ghost hearse usually vanishes when it reaches the cemetery.

Bloody Bluff Road is a haven for birdwatchers. Driving down the winding road, one can catch fleeting glimpses of a variety of sparrows, including swamp, chirping, Bachman's and song sparrows. Yellow-throated warblers, blue-headed vireos and swallow-tailed and Mississippi kites can be seen at the end of the road. However, teenagers travel down the Bloody Bluff Road late at night in the hope of being pursued by the fabled Ghost Hearse of Sumatra.

10
TALLAHASSEE

VELDA MOUND

The Fort Walton peoples constructed Velda Mound in Leon Country probably around 1450. Their descendants, the Apalachee, continued living here throughout most of the sixteenth century. The area, which also included the Lake Jackson Mounds, was called "Apalachee Province" by the Spanish explorers. The Indian village surrounded the platform mound, which was reserved as a residence for the village leader. By 1565, the Indians had abandoned Velda Mound, probably because the soil and the forests had been depleted. After they left the area, neither the Spanish nor the British colonists occupied the mound. In the 1950s, Velda Mound and the surrounding area became grazing land for the Velda Dairy company. The mound was damaged during this time by looters, who dug into the structure. Eventually, a real estate developer purchased the land for the purposes of building subdivisions there. Today, the mound, which has been purchased and restored by the State of Florida, sits, incongruously, in the Arbor Hill neighborhood, which is situated inside the Killearn Estates subdivision.

People living in Ann Arbor have reported a number of eerie occurrences over the years. A glowing white wolf has been seen loping around the mound. Spectral howling echoes through the neighborhood occasionally. A small group of phantom Indians has been seen sitting around a campfire on the mound. Witnesses say the Indians are visible for only a few seconds before they fade away. Shadowlike figures are occasionally spotted walking around a corner of the mound, accompanied by a bright flash of light. Fast-moving shadow people have also been sighted running into the woods or across the street. Most of the sightings of apparitions occur during the summer months. People living close to the mounds have had strange things happen in their houses. For example, a man walked into his garage one night and was surprised that his bicycle light had turned itself on. Although rational explanations have been offered for most of this seemingly paranormal activity, passersby cannot walk or drive past Velda Mound without feeling as if they are being watched.

GOODWOOD MUSEUM AND GARDENS

Hardy Croom was a lawyer, planter and amateur botanist who established a farm around Tallahassee in the 1830s. He is known today for the discovery of a rare tree that he found growing in Bristol, Florida, in 1834. Croom contacted botanist Dr. John Torrey at Columbia College. Torrey declared the tree a species that once grew worldwide before the last ice age. Croom believed that these were the fabled gopherwood trees in the Bible that supplied the wood for Noah's ark. The scientific name for these trees, which are found only in Bristol, is *Torreyan taxifolia*.

In 1835, Hardy Croom began building a magnificent home for himself, his wife, Frances, and their children. He named the house Goodwood. In October 1837, he was bringing the family back from North Carolina on the steamship SS *Home*. The ship was lost in a terrible storm, and Croom and his family drowned. Hardy's brother, Bryan, and his wife, Eveline Croom, inherited Goodwood. Bryan immediately set about completing the Main House. He also planted cotton, corn and sweet potatoes. However, Bryan and Eveline soon became embroiled in a lawsuit with Frances Croom's mother, Henrietta Smith. After a court battle that lasted twenty years, Mrs. Smith won and sold the house to Arvah and Susan Hopkins, who turned the house into the social center of Tallahassee between the 1850s and 1880s. In 1865, after the Union army captured Tallahassee, the Hopkins reluctantly entertained Federal officers in their home.

Following the death of her husband in 1885, Mrs. Hopkins sold Goodwood to an Englishman, Dr. William Lamb Arrowsmith, and his wife, Elizabeth. Dr. Arrowsmith died within a few months of taking ownership of the estate, so Elizabeth occupied herself by planting beds of daffodils

Goodwood Mansion was built in the early 1830s by a native of North Carolina named Hardy Croom.

on the west lawn in front of the driveway. She also had a large arrow of paved bricks made in the ground. She wanted the arrow to point south to, in her words, "make people ponder."

Elizabeth Arrowsmith remained at Goodwood for twenty-five years before finally selling it in 1911 to a wealthy widow named Mrs. Alexander Tiers. Fanny Tiers, whose principal residence was in Morris County, New Jersey, immediately set about expanding the estate. She built several guest cottages and a large swimming pool on the property. She also had a water tank constructed in the backyard. Gravitational flow provided water for the faucets and toilets. Fanny was also responsible for the general Colonial Revival design of the gardens. Because Goodwood was one of the first homes in Tallhassee to have electric lights, large crowds formed around the house whenever Fanny turned on the lights at night.

In 1925, Margaret Hodges, the wife of Senator William C. Hodges, sent her husband to Goodwood to buy an antique bed. Fanny refused to sell the bed separately, but she did agree to sell Hodges the house and all the furnishings, including the bed. During parties that the senator and his wife held at Goodwood, he often remarked that this was the most expensive bed

71

Docents standing in front of this fireplace have felt a ghostly presence standing behind them. *Photo courtesy of Marilyn Brown.*

in Florida. Hodges also bought back some of the original furniture that had been sold by some of the previous owners to pay their legal bills. One of William Hodges's pet projects was the expansion of the garden. All of the plants in the garden today are taken from Hodges's 1929 inventory. In a high-profile trial, William Hodges defended a local woman named Dixie Goad for the murder of her husband in 1930.

In 1940, Senator Hodges died, but Margaret continued to entertain at her luxurious home. One of the guests who visited Goodwood was renowned writer Helen Keller. In 1948, Margaret married one of the men who rented one of her guest cottages, an army officer named Thomas M. Hood. He was an artist who painted the daisies, roses and grapes on the ceilings and walls of the house. By the 1970s, the house was becoming increasingly difficult to maintain, but Margaret insisted that Goodwood was "too precious to part with." Before his death in 1990, Thomas M. Hood established the Margaret E. Wilson Foundation in memory of his wife to preserve Goodwood. Today, Goodwood Museum and Gardens, Inc. has assumed stewardship of Goodwood.

Although Goodwood is known primarily as one of the most beautiful historic homes in Tallahassee, it is gradually becoming known among paranormal enthusiasts as a very haunted place as well. In her book *Hauntings in Florida's Panhandle*, author Nicole Carlson Easley chronicled some of the ghostly activity that has occurred inside the old house. Easley said that volunteers who stand in front of the fireplace in the dining room have felt the unmistakable presence of someone standing directly behind them. Docents and guests have experienced sudden drops of temperature while walking through parts of the house. Volunteers who were cataloguing items inside the house one day reported feeling very cold when they picked up specific objects. Goodwood, it seems, is a place where the previous owners still make claim to their property, even from the "other side."

SUNLAND MENTAL HOSPITAL

In 1952, a chain of hospitals called the W.T. Edwards Tuberculosis Hospitals opened up in Tallahassee, Marianna, Lantana, Tampa, Miami and a number of other cities in south Florida. The W.T. Edwards Tuberculosis Hospital in Tallahassee was located at the corner of Phillips Road and Blair Stone Road. Small wings branched off from the narrow, five-story-high main buildings. Multi-pane windows, which could be opened by means of cranks, provided fresh air for the benefit of the patients. Windows also blanketed the back of the main buildings. After a cure for tuberculosis was discovered in the early 1960s, the facilities were taken over by the Florida Department of Health. In 1968, they were converted into Sunland Hospitals for Mentally Impaired Children. In the 1970s, patient care began to decline as a result of the shortage of government funds. In 1978, the Association of Retarded Citizens filed a class action lawsuit against the hospital, alleging patient neglect. The abundance of asbestos in the facility also contributed to the closing of the four-hundred-bed hospital in 1983.

The seeds of ghost legends circulating around Sunland Mental Hospital were planted long before it shut its doors. Whispered accounts of secret lobotomies were passed around for many years, despite the absence of surgical facilities. Patients were said to be physically abused inside the hospital. Sexual abuse was also said to take place behind the closed doors of the hospital. The rumors concerning the use of shock therapy proved to be true though. In fact, Tallahassee's Sunland Mental Hospital was the first in the state to employ shock therapy in the treatment of seizures. However, the fabled use of lobotomies to treat unruly patients was never verified.

During the two decades when the old hospital stood vacant, it served as a place of shelter for rodents and vagrants and as a playground for vandals. Teenagers began prowling around the dark recesses of the abandoned building in search of parties and any verification of the ghost stories that had lured them there. Young people told terrifying tales of hearing childish laughter, shuffling sounds and ghostly whispers throughout the entire building. Reports of bizarre lights on the upper stories were commonplace. Some people reported hearing the bouncing of a ball in the gloomy hallways. Many trespassers reported hearing objects being dropped on the floor and the breaking of glass. The scuffing sound of shoes on the floor and the soft voices of people deep in conversation, like doctors and nurses, frequently echoed through the hallways. Unexplained lights were frequently sighted through vacant windows in the building long after the electricity had been turned off. One of the trespassers heard a loud crash that sounded as if someone had dropped a metal tray. Teenagers spoke of getting the "shivers" while passing through the various cold spots in the building. People have caught a glimpse of the apparition of a little boy running around corners in the hallway. The squeaky sounds of a gurney being pushed down the hallway have raised goose bumps on the arm of young visitors. One particularly terrified youngster said he heard loud screams and felt as if he was enveloped in a vortex of anger. People passing by the outside of the old building reported hearing muffled cries, and cold spots appeared throughout the building. In his book *Florida's Ghostly Legends and Haunted Folklore: Volume 2,* author Greg Jenkins said many visitors experienced a drastic drop in temperature as they walked past the steel cages where unruly children were kept. Jenkins also said that the ghost of a dog that had been used in "pet therapy" sessions with children was a presence inside the building for many years. People reported hearing the whimper of a large dog; they also said they could hear the jingling of dog tags as it ran down the hallway.

In the 1900s and 2000s, the ghost tales caught the attention of paranormal investigators. Countless orbs and misty, shadowy shapes have been photographed in the hospital. A number of startling EVPS, including the sounds of a bouncing ball and spectral voices, have been recorded inside the hospital. One group even caught the image of a small boy bouncing a ball down the hallway.

The dilapidated building was finally razed in 2006. Today, the site is occupied by the Victoria Grand Apartments, where guests entertain themselves by swimming in the pools and exercising in the workout facilities, completely oblivious to the death and misery suffered by hundreds of tuberculosis patients and innocent children.

JEFFERSON CORRECTIONAL INSTITUTION

Prisons have always had the reputation of being ideal locations for spirit activity. Yuma Territorial Prison, Idaho State Penitentiary, the Mansfield Reformatory and the West Virginia State Penitentiary are just a few of the haunted penal institutions that immediately come to mind. Of course, Alcatraz has the highest profile among all the haunted prisons, probably because it housed such well-known criminals as Al Capone and Robert Stroud ("The Birdman of Alcatraz"). Interestingly enough, though, not all haunted prisons are those that have been deactivated. According to many inmates and guards, something otherworldly is locked behind the gates of the Jefferson Correctional Institution.

The Jefferson Correctional Institution was originally built as a prison for male inmates. However, in 1990, it was converted to a women's prison.

Then in October 1999, the Jefferson Correction Institution became a men's prison once again. The prison, which can house up to 1,179 inmates, has seven open bay housing units and one cell housing unit. The prison offers no vocational programs, but inmates can receive Adult Basic Education and General Educational Development (GED) inside the prison walls. Institutional betterment programs offered by the prison include Alcoholics Anonymous, Better's Intervention, Fresh Start Smoking Cessation, Active and Passive Sports, Wellness Education and a Law Library Program.

In many ways, the Jefferson Correctional Institution is a state-of-the-art detention facility. However, accounts given by a number of guards and inmates indicate that sometimes, elements from the past make their presence known, mostly because the prison is rumored to have been built on top of an abandoned graveyard. Female inmates claimed to have been tapped by phantom fingers while they were asleep. Ghostly children have been sighted playing in the dorms late at night. One inmate swears that he saw an eight-foot-tall angel in Dorm G. Guards taking a stroll through the prison late at night have heard keys hitting the bars when they were the only ones in the area. The ghost of a little girl has been seen several times sitting outside one of the cells. A few inmates reported seeing a man sitting astride a horse in the prison yard late at night.

The Florida Department of Corrections operates the third-largest state prison system in the United States, with over 102,000 inmates incarcerated and over 27,000 employees. Because the major crime rate dropped 52 percent from 1991 to 2010, three prisons, two boot camps and one road prison were closed in the first quarter of 2011. In March 2012, Jefferson Correctional Institution was removed from the list of seven prisons and four work camps slated to be closed. County leaders were ecstatic because closing the prison would have cost the community more than $30 million in jobs and lost revenues. Many ghost hunters, on the other hand, are looking forward to the day when the prison finally closes so that they can investigate the institution's ghosts without having to be incarcerated first.

THE OLD LEON COUNTY JAIL

Of all the places likely to be harboring ghosts, jails and prisons are at the top of the list. Haunted jails are so common within the South that they have been featured in countless books, documentaries and ghost tours. In

Charleston, South Caroline, the Old City Jail, which was opened in 1802, is said to be inhabited by the lost souls of slaves, pirates and Civil War prisoners. The Jailer's Inn in Bardstown, Kentucky, was built in 1819. It is haunted by the spirit of Martin Hill, who murdered his wife at his neighbor's house. Even jails of a more recent vintage have had their share of paranormal activity. On October 27, 2012, this writer encountered an interactive spirit in Meridian, Mississippi's abandoned City Jail, which was added to the top floor of the Lauderdale County Courthouse in 1939. This seemed to be the ghost of a convict who had hanged himself on the upper floor. The Old Leon County Jail in Tallahassee is unique among haunted jails in that some of its ghosts are clearly malevolent spirits.

The Old Leon County Jail is on Calhoun Street near its intersection with Pensacola Street. Constructed in the 1930s, this box-like building served as the county's primary detention facility until the 1950s, when a new jail was built closer to the police station. "Over-flow prisoners" continued to be housed in the old jail until the 1960s, when it was acquired by the Florida State Archives as a storage unit. In the 1990s, the Department of Revenue moved into the former jail.

Although the building did not serve as a jail for very long, it saw more than its share of brutality. Most of the prisoners, who were primarily African Americans or indigent whites, were physically abused by the guards and, frequently, by each other. Extremely dangerous criminals were often placed in the same jail cell. An untold number of inmates died at their own hands or those of someone else inside the old jail.

Strong evidence exists that the building's violent past has somehow imprinted itself in the walls and floors. After the building was turned over to the Florida State Archives, people working by themselves late into the night in the 1970s reported hearing doors slamming, even though there was no one else inside the building at the time. Archivists working in the rooms that had been converted from the old jail cells claimed to have heard spectral voices after dark. In the 1980s, an archivist heard footsteps proceeding through an empty room. Another employee had an even more terrifying experience when he heard what seemed like a large sledgehammer pounding an inner wall. He was confused because no remodeling had been scheduled at the time. After the pounding stopped, he walked into the room and checked out the wall where the pounding had taken place. The wall was entirely blemish-free.

In his book *Haunting Sunshine*, author Jack Powell says that the same man who heard the eerie pounding had another weird experience inside the building. Once again, he was working by himself late at night. At 2:30

a.m., he heard strange noises coming from another room, so he decided to investigate. He was walking down the hallway and had just turned a corner when he noticed one of the old jailhouse doors slowly swing open by itself. After staying open for a few seconds, the door slowly closed. The archivist later told his supervisor that even though the air conditioning unit was blowing full-blast at the time, the force of the air was not strong enough to move an iron door weighing over one hundred pounds.

The paranormal activity inside the Old Leon County Jail peaked in the mid- to late 1980s, following the discovery of the Spanish treasure ship *Atocha* near the Marquesas Keys on June 20, 1985. While the courts deliberated the rightful ownership of the treasure, the gold, jewels and other priceless artifacts were stored in the former Leon County Jail, primarily because it was the most secure location in the immediate area. Ed Fausel, a local archaeologist who was very familiar with the storage of the *Atocha*'s treasure, said that while the artifacts were being held in the old jail, one very violent incident occurred. An archaeologist was walking up the staircase late one night when a pair of invisible arms picked him up and hurled him down the steps. Fortunately, he was not seriously injured.

The ghosts inside the Old Leon County Jail seem to have settled down since the Department of Revenue moved in. Even though a number of structural changes were made in the 1990s, including the addition of two wings and a parking lot, the removal of a carport and the creation of a lovely garden, nothing seems to have "stirred up" the spirits in recent years. Perhaps they attached themselves to some of the objects that were stored here by the Florida Department of Archives.

OAKLAND CEMETERY

Oakland Cemetery is nestled in Tallahassee's Frenchtown area at 312 West Brevard Street. With graves dating back to the 1850s, Oakland Cemetery is the second-oldest cemetery in Tallahassee. It served as the largest African American cemetery in the city during the last half of the nineteenth century and the first half of the twentieth century. The cemetery's 1,500 graves are the final resting place of some of Tallahassee's most illustrious citizens. Claude Denson Pepper (1990–1989) served as Democratic senator from Florida to the United States Senate from 1936 to 1951. He served in the U.S. House of Representatives from 1963 until 1989. Alva Thomas

Yon (1882–1971) represented Florida's Third District in the U.S. House of Representatives from 1927 to 1933. PGA golfer Bert Yancey (1938–1994) was one of the country's top golfers from the mid-1960s to the early 1970s. The graves of 187 veterans can be found at Oakland Cemetery as well. The last burial in Oakland Cemetery took place in 1998. One of the historic cemetery's greatest attractions is its collection of funerary art, which includes picturesque inscriptions on tombstones and elaborate tombs.

Without a doubt, the most famous tomb in Oakland Cemetery is the sepulcher of an eccentric character named Calvin C. Phillips. The twenty-foot-high structure, which was the first tomb erected in the cemetery, is also distinctive because of the minaret placed on top of the vault. After his tomb was built in the early 1900s, Phillips had his custom-made cherry wood coffin carried inside. He gave a friend the key to the tomb with instructions to lock it up after he passed away. Legend has it that Phillips, sensing that he was about to die, climbed inside his new coffin and died. According to Dennis William Hauck, author of *Haunted Places: The National Directory*, people who visit Phillips's unique tomb experience "weird feelings."

THE LIVELY BUILDING

Constructed in 1875 at 200 South Monroe Street, the Lively Building is one of the city's most historic structures. Its name is derived from Matthew Lively, a pharmacist who operated a drugstore on the first floor. The top floor was used as offices. The Lively Building acquired a somewhat notorious reputation when the Leon Bar opened up on the first floor in 1892.

Many of the Leon Bar's customers were a rowdy bunch of cowboys known as the Florida Crackers. These nomadic cowboys, who could trace their lineage back to the Scotch-Irish and English settlers, made their living working the Pineywoods cattle that roamed the Florida woods. These free-ranging cows were descended from the hardy breed of cattle left behind by the Spanish explorers in the fifteenth and sixteenth centuries. They thrived in the wilds of Florida because of their natural resistance to the indigenous diseases and parasites. The Crackers, who were as tough as the cattle they drove, differed from the cowboy of the American Southwest in that they used cow whips and dogs instead of lassos to herd cattle. On payday, a large number of these men could be found "whooping it up" at the Leon Bar, where they drank beer and whiskey and cavorted with

The Lively Building, which was built in 1975, is haunted by the rowdy ghosts of Crackers.

loose women. Shootings and stabbings were common occurrences at this "Wild West"–type saloon. An untold number of people are said to have been murdered there.

The Leon Bar was closed in 1904—not by the local police, but by a local ordinance prohibiting the sale of liquor within the city limits. Tallahassee was one of many cities that was affected by the temperance movement, which encouraged moderation or the prohibition of alcoholic spirits. The temperance movement was driven mostly by women, most notably Susan B. Anthony, Frances E. Willard and Carry A. Nation. Temperance workers described saloons like the Leon Bar as "enticing [places] where our boys may drink in style and elegance amidst strains of dreamy music and all that gilds and sugarcoats sin." The efforts of the temperance movement eventually resulted in government regulation of alcohol and the passing of the Eighteenth Amendment.

The Leon Bar is long gone, and so are the Florida Crackers, whose freewheeling lifestyle could not withstand the encroachments of civilization. The Pineywoods cattle that supplied them with a living have been placed on the "critical" list by the American Livestock Breeds Conservancy. Apparitions of lanky, bearded young men wearing leather chaps and wide-brimmed hats have been sighted lounging around the corner where the bright lights of the Leon Bar once beckoned to thirsty souls eager to spend their hard-earned money and forget about the rigors of their lives for a while.

THE KNOTT HOUSE

Luella and William Knott were one of Tallahassee's most prominent couples in the first half of the twentieth century. Luella, who was born in Graham, North Carolina, on May 31, 1871, became an orphan at age six following the death of her parents from tuberculosis. She graduated from Greensboro Methodist College in 1891. Her husband, William Knott, was born in Terrell County, Georgia, on November 24, 1863. While growing up, William helped his father in the family's citrus grove near Leesburg. As an adult, William partnered with his brother Charles and started a phosphate mining business near Ocala. Later, William enjoyed success as an accountant and a civil servant. William met Luella in central Florida, where she was teaching school. The couple was married in 1895 and moved to Tallahassee two years later. At the time, William was working as the state financial agent. He became the state's first state auditor under Governor Jennings's administration. When Sidney Catts became governor in 1917, William returned to agriculture. He also accepted the position of head administrator of the state hospital in Chattahoochee. In 1927, William was once again appointed state auditor under Governor John Martin.

Because William was working for the state once again, he and Luella returned to Tallahassee. In 1928, they moved into the house that is now the Knott House Museum. A year later, William replaced John Luning as state treasurer and held that position under two more governors. He retired at age seventy-five.

At the same time that William was building his political career, Luella occupied herself as a mother, poet and social activist. When she was not homeschooling the couple's three children, she found time to lead a campaign against the consumption of alcohol in Florida. Because she was the wife of an important state official, Luella felt obligated to entertain at her home. She frequently tied her poems to the furnishings during these parties to attract her guests' attention to her antiques. Luella died on April 11, 1965; her husband had preceded her in death only eight days earlier.

The Knott House was built in 1843 by an African American contractor named George Proctor for attorney Thomas Hagner.

Luella and William were not the only occupants of the house at 301 East Park Avenue. George Proctor built the house in 1843 for a lawyer named Thomas Hagner, who presented it as a wedding gift to his wife, Catherine Gamble. Following her husband's death two years later, Catherine turned the home into a boardinghouse. In 1865, toward the end of the Civil War, Brigadier General Edward McCook read the Emancipation Proclamation from the porch. Dr. George Betton purchased the house in 1883 and set up a clinic in the basement. Following Dr. Betton's death in the house in 1896, another doctor, Dr. John W. Scott, moved into the house with his wife, Caroline Scott, in 1919. He died in the house in 1920, eight years before Luella and William Knott moved in.

The last person to live in the Knott House was Luella and William's son, Charlie. He inherited the house in 1965 following his parents' deaths and

Opposite, top: Visitors to the Knott House have sensed energy emanating from the books in this library.

Opposite, bottom: A visitor saw a male apparition in this bedroom in the Knott House.

remained there until his death in 1985. A year later, the house was acquired by the Tallahassee Preservation Board, which operated it as a museum. It was opened to the public in 1992.

Because so many people have died in the Knott House, it is small wonder that locals found it easy to believe that it was haunted. A photograph depicting was appears to be the ghostly image of a human being is on display inside the house. It was taken by one of the staff members. In her book *Hauntings in Florida's Panhandle*, author Nicole Carlson Easley says that a staff member who was working in her office late one evening heard someone walking up and down the stairs. She became frightened when she realized that the young woman she was working with had gone home for the day. Several staff members have heard someone walking around the second floor when it was supposed to be empty at the time.

Visitors to the Knott House have also had some very strange encounters. People participating in the museum's "Real Ghost House" tour have reported walking into parts of the old house that are unusually cold. A few guests have sensed large amounts of psychic energy emanating from the bookcase. A visitor claimed to have caught a glimpse of a male apparition in one of the upper bedrooms of the house. According to author Nicole Carlson Easley, one guest claimed to have seen a group of women wearing antebellum dresses in the living room. They may have been the spirits of some of Luella's friends, who often wore nineteenth-century dresses during specific social functions. The legacy of Luella and William Knox, it seems, is of the ethereal as well as the material kind.

FLORIDA STATE UNIVERSITY

The earliest beginnings of Florida State University can be traced back to 1851 when the West Florida Seminary was founded. The University offered classes from 1857 to 1863, when its name was changed to the Florida Military and Collegiate Institute. The cadets who were trained there distinguished themselves during the Battle of Natural Bridge. In fact, these young soldiers are credited with making Tallahassee the only Confederate capital east of the Mississippi River that did not fall to the Union army. In 1865, after the South surrendered, the Federal forces were stationed on the campus of the Florida Military and Collegiate Institute.

The institute continued to grow and evolve after the Civil War. In 1901, the institution, which had become the first liberal arts college in Florida,

This decorative fountain at the entrance of Florida State University stands on the site of a hanging place called "Gallows Hill."

changed its name again to Florida State College. In 1905, the four-year institution became Florida Female College. Males were not readmitted until 1947 to accommodate the influx of veterans who were enrolling in college on the G.I. Bill. That same year, the legislature changed the institution's name to Florida State University. During the 1950s, a number of new colleges were added, including the College of Arts and Science, the College of Education, the College of Business and the College of Nursing. The first black student was admitted in 1962. In 2001, a College of Medicine was established on the campus. By 2011, Florida State University had expanded to 542 buildings on 1,550 acres.

Florida State University has clearly taken its place among the major academic and research institutions in the United States. Through the years, the university has also acquired a reputation for being haunted. In fact, some people believe that the university was destined to become haunted from the very beginning. In the 1800s, the location on which the university was founded was known as "Gallows Hill." Convicted criminals were chained and shackled and lifted onto an ox cart. They were then transported to the gallows, where they were hanged in full view of hundreds of people. Afterward, the corpses of the criminals were placed on the same ox cart and carried over to the cemetery. Today, a beautiful fountain stands in the same place where hundreds of prisoners were executed, but the misery of the people who died there has not been totally erased. Students walking past the fountain report hearing ghostly moans floating through the air, even when no one else is present.

Like most colleges and universities in the South, Florida State University also has haunted dormitories. Cawthon Hall is a 297-bed co-ed suite-style residence hall. It is said to be haunted by the ghost of a young woman who was sunbathing on a balcony on the roof when she fell asleep. Suddenly, black clouds rolled across the sky. A few minutes later, a bolt of lightning struck the sleeping girl, killing her instantly. Students living in the girl's former room claim to have heard weird sounds at night. Objects placed on a table or chair during the day are moved to an entirely different spot the next day. Residents living in different rooms have also had strange experiences. Lights have been known to turn on and off by themselves. The faint strains of music occasionally waft through the air. Spectral voices have been heard in empty rooms. A student who was walking down the hallway reported seeing a door hanger placed on one of the doors by the resident assistant shaking on its own.

The ghost haunting Reynolds Hall, a 247-bed co-ed dormitory, is less well known but just as terrifying. Students say that years ago, a janitor hanged himself in Reynolds Hall. Ever since then, students living in the residence hall have experienced poltergeist activity. Doors open and close on their own. Showers turn off and on when no one is present. Students have been awakened by the rattling of glasses and bottles in the bathroom.

Some—if not most—of the deaths that are said to have occurred at Florida State University and other colleges and universities are probably apocryphal. However, Florida State University became an actual murder site in the early morning hours of January 15, 1978. Some time after midnight, serial killer Ted Bundy boldly walked into the Chi Omega sorority house. He severely injured two young women and bludgeoned and strangled two others to death. The officer at the scene, FSU Police Sergeant Bill Taylor said that when he walked up the stairs, he found Karen Chandler at the top. She told Sergeant Taylor that she and her roommate, Kathy Kleiner, had been attacked by a strange man. Sergeant Taylor's fellow officer, Ray Crew, found Margaret Bowman beaten to death in her room. He then walked across the hall to Lisa Levy's room and found that the young woman had stopped breathing. Crew and the EMTs tried unsuccessfully to revive her. Lisa Levy had been sexually assaulted, beaten on the head with a log and strangled. Afterward, police learned that Bundy had walked a few blocks to a home on Dunwoody Street that had been converted into apartments and attacked a fifth woman. In his book *Haunted Places: A National Directory*, author Dennis William Hauck says that a sorority girl told crime writer Ann Rule that on the night of the murders, she was about to get out of bed and get a drink of water, but something compelled her not to open the door. In the years that followed the grisly attacks, many sorority girls reported feeling uncomfortable inside the sorority house. Some believe that the Chi Omega Sorority House is haunted by the spirits of the two girls who were murdered there.

When Ted Bundy arrived in Tallahassee after escaping from jail in Colorado, the Phi Delta Theta fraternity house was a rooming house called "The Oak." He rented a room in the apartment house and set about forging a new identity. His plans for getting a job and starting a new life ended abruptly after the January 15, 1978 attack at the Chi Omega Sorority house. Bundy was apprehended, tried and executed in Florida's electric chair on January 24, 1989. In his book *Haunted Places: The National Directory*, author Dennis William Hauck said that a few weeks after Bundy was executed, two young women walking past The Oak saw a handsome young man matching Ted Bundy's description standing on the front porch. Some people believe that Ted Bundy's ghost returned to The Oak because this apartment house was the last place where Ted Bundy felt good about the direction his life was about to take.

FLORIDA HISTORIC CAPITOL MUSEUM

Florida's first state capitol was built in 1826, but it was razed in 1839 before construction was completed. Six years later, the second state capitol was built, just before Florida was admitted into the Union. In 1902, architect Frank Millburn made the first addition to the state capitol. In 1923, architect Henry Klutho created the building's marble interior and added two wings. In 1936, a wing for the House chamber was built. Eleven years later, the Senate chamber was added on. By the early 1970s, plans were being made to demolish the Old State Capitol. However, a group of concerned citizens saved the historic structure from the wrecking ball. Between 1978 and 1982, the Old State Capitol was restored to its 1902 appearance. Today, the old building houses the Florida Legislative Research Center and Museum on the ground floor. Not only can assorted collections of photographs, papers and oral histories be found here, but so can the ghost of a former governor.

John Milton, the fifth governor of Florida, was born in Louisville, Georgia. He attended law school and practiced law in Georgia and Alabama. After moving to New Orleans for a short time, he decided to make Florida his

Florida Historic Capitol Museum is haunted by the ghost of Governor John Milton, who committed suicide toward the end of the Civil War.

permanent home in 1846. He served as presidential elector for the State of Florida in 1848 before being elected to the Florida House of Representatives two years later. In 1860, he was elected governor of the State of Florida. An ardent secessionist, Milton was fully supportive of the Southern cause during the Civil War. He saw to it that his state became one of the Confederacy's major suppliers of salt and food. As the Civil War drew to a close, Milton sank into depression. He left the governor's mansion in Tallahassee and moved back to his plantation, Sylvania, in Marianna, Florida. After giving his final speech to the state legislature, Milton went home and shot himself in the head on April 1, 1865.

The tragic legacy of Governor John Milton still resonates within the building where he did his best to guide the destiny of the state he loved so much. For many years, people have heard disembodied footsteps. Doors open and close on their own. A male voice has been heard in rooms where nobody is present. Many people believe that John Milton is the spirit responsible for the ghostly occurrences in the Old State Capitol because in his final speech, he proclaimed that "death would be preferable to reunion."

THE OLD CITY CEMETERY

The Old City Cemetery is the oldest graveyard in Tallassee. When it was established in 1829 by the Territorial legislature, Tallahassee had been the state capital for only five years. At the time, the cemetery was located outside of the city, which was still a heavily wooded area, populated by brigands and ruffians. The cemetery was nearly as wild as Tallahassee. Wild hogs and other animals rooted through the graveyard, which was unkempt, for the most part. Tallahassee acquired the cemetery in 1840. The city sectioned it off in a system of squares following the Yellow Fever Epidemic of 1841, which claimed between 230 and 400 victims. African Americans were interred in the western half of the cemetery, and whites were buried in the eastern half. Many families had their own plots, which were bordered by wrought-iron fences. The earliest graves were marked by wooden crosses, many of which have rotted away. A two-hundred-foot clearing on the far side of the cemetery protected Tallahassee from attacks by Native Americans.

During the Civil War, both Confederate and Union soldiers were buried in the Old City Cemetery. Many of the Confederate soldiers were killed during the Battle of Olustee, not far from Lake City. Most of the Union soldiers in

The Old City Cemetery is the oldest public burial ground in Tallahassee.

the cemetery were killed in the Battle of Natural Bridge. A number of the Union casualties were African Americans. Most of these grave markers bear the simple inscription "U.S. Soldier." In her book *Fifteen Florida Cemeteries*, author Lola Haskins says that the corpses of twenty-three Union soldiers were moved from the Old City Cemetery to burial grounds in Beaufort, South Carolina, in 1866 by an enterprising businessman named J.P. Low, who charged their loved ones $8.00 per body.

A number of changes were made to the Old City Cemetery around the turn of the century. In 1890, a special section of consecrated ground was reserved for Jewish people, some of whom have been removed to Jacksonville, Florida. During the 1890s, the United Daughters of the Confederacy erected a platform that is still used today during commemorations and on Confederate Memorial Day. Since the 1870s, flowers have been placed on the graves of Confederate and Union soldiers during the services.

The last burial plot in the Old City Cemetery was sold in 1902. Today, the seven-acre cemetery is completely full. The places that appear to be devoid of graves contain bodies marked by wooden crosses and "tombstones," all of which rotted away many years ago. Throughout most of the twentieth century, the cemetery was neglected. In the 1980s, vandals caused considerable damage to many of the tombstones. In 1991, most of the damaged tombstones were restored with funds provided by the Florida Department of State. The Historic Tallahassee Preservation Board also sponsored the elaborate undertaking. Unfortunately, a number of other tombstones were damaged in the years following the restoration.

Some of the city's most prestigious founders are interred in the Old City Cemetery. In the African American section, one can find the grave of Dr. William J. Gunn. He was the first African American resident of Florida to graduate from medical school. Dr. Gunn spent his entire career practicing medicine in Tallahassee. One of the most illustrious black families in Tallahassee also has a plot in the African American section: the Proctor family. One member of this family, John Proctor, not only became a druggist, but he also served in Florida's House and Senate. Florida's first ordained black Baptist minister, James Paige, can be found here as well.

The occupants of several of the graves in the white section are also important figures in the history of Tallahassee. The earliest stone tombstone is that of Daniel Lynes, a merchant from New York City who died on a visit to Tallahassee. Thomas Brown, the governor of Florida from 1849 to 1853, is buried here. Undoubtedly, though, the most famous grave in the Old City Cemetery is that of Elizabeth Budd Graham. Bessie, as she was known to her friends, died in 1889 when she was only twenty-three years old. She was survived by a husband and two small children. Her tomb is one of the grandest in the entire cemetery. It is adorned with large granite vases and feathers carved from stone. She was, by all accounts, a loving mother and wife whose loss was sorely felt by her family.

However, over the years, Bessie Graham has acquired the reputation of being a witch. She was born in October, the same month during which Halloween is observed. The placement of her monument has also led to speculation that she was in league with the devil. In many communities, Christians are buried facing the east so that on Judgment Day, they can meet Jesus Christ, who will arrive with the rising sun. However, a number of upstanding citizens are also buried facing the west in Old City Cemetery, providing evidence that she was not a witch. People who are convinced that Bessie Graham was a wicked woman also point to the inscription, taken from Edgar Allan Poe's poem "Lenore." They argue that her connection to America's master of the macabre points to her "dark side." This charge also seems to be contradicted by another inscription on her tombstone, "No Cross No Crown," the title of a religious devotional

This lavish monument marks the grave of a witch, Elizabeth "Bessie" Graham.

written by William Penn in 1669. The inscription indicates the soul's spiritual victory over the world.

Bessie Graham will always be thought of as a witch in Tallahassee, probably because legends are often much more fascinating than historical fact. Some people say that she was interred in such an elaborate tomb because she bewitched a rich man to marry her and to arrange for her to be buried in grand style. Others claim to have been touched by icy fingers while gazing at her tomb. It is small wonder that Bessie Graham's tomb is the most visited grave in the Old City Cemetery.

THE COLUMNS

The magnificent two-and-a-half story Greek Revival mansion at 100 North Duval Street was built in 1830 by a banker named William W. "Money" Williams, the first president of the Bank of Florida. Legend has it that Williams earned the nickname "Money" when he arrived in

This Greek Revival mansion, the Columns, is said to be haunted by the ghost of a woman whose husband never returned from the Civil War.

Tallahassee with a wagonload of cash. Williams, his wife and their ten children lived in the main house. The bank was housed in a wing on the side of the house.

Another occupant of the Columns was Benjamin Chaires, whose brick factory probably produced the hundreds of bricks used in the building of the mansion. Although Chaires did not own the mansion, he signed the deed as president of the Union Bank, which owned the house at the time. Chaires and his family were not permanent residents of the house; they lived there only at those times when attacks by hostile Indians were imminent.

In 1971, the Columns was moved to its present location at the corner of Pike Avenue and Duval Street. It is the oldest surviving residential building with the original city limits of Tallahassee. Over the years, it has served as a school and as the James Madison Institute. Today, the chamber of commerce is housed inside the Columns, which is as renowned for its legends as it is for its distinctive architecture.

One of these legends concerns the bricks themselves. Back when the Columns was used as a school, students began spreading rumors that

"Money" Williams had stuck nickels in the mortar between every brick in the building. For years, students scraped out the mortar in the hopes of uncovering the buried nickels.

Another legend connected with the old house concerns a young married couple who resided there during the Civil War. The story goes that one day, the husband informed his wife that he had enlisted in the Confederate army. The next day, with tears streaming down her cheeks, the woman waved good-bye as her husband rode off to war. For the next several months, she eagerly awaited the arrival of letters from her brave soldier, but she never heard from him again. Some people believe that the distraught woman still occupies the house where she had waited so long, in vain, for her husband to return. The most commonly reported paranormal occurrence inside the house is the apparition of a woman who enters and leaves the large fireplace on the first floor. Apparently, she is one of those mournful spirits whose search for her lost love has extended far beyond death.

11

WASHINGTON COUNTY

THE FIDDLING GHOST OF BOYNTON ISLAND

Boynton Island was created by sediment deposited by the Choctawhatchee River. Holmes Creek drains into the river at the foot of the island. Boynton Island is a strange, ghostly place replete with legends. One of these tales concerns a huge alligator that could knock a mule into the water with a swipe of its tail that ravaged livestock throughout southern Alabama in the 1920s. Apparently, it moved to northwestern Florida after a farmer named Pap Haines tried unsuccessfully to kill it by tossing dynamite in a pond. The demonic alligator became known regionally as "Two-Toed Tom" because it had lost two of its toes in a steel trap. In the 1980s, reports surfaced of a monstrous alligator between eighteen and twenty-four feet long sunning itself on a sand bar near Boynton Island.

Two-Toed Tom is not the only entity on Boynton Island that seems to be able to defy death. Another folkloric denizen of Boynton Island is a phantom fiddler named Moses Boynton. Census records of 1860 indicate that he hailed from Alabama and was the head of a household on Boynton Island. In 1864, he enlisted in the Confederate army and served a few months in Company C, Eleventh Florida Infantry, before being dropped from the active rolls. No one knows for sure if he was honorably discharged or if he deserted, as so many Confederate soldiers did toward the end of the war. The fact is that a number of Confederate deserters did use Boynton Island as a hiding place. If Moses Boynton was not actually affiliated with these men, he seems to have arrived at some kind of understanding with them.

In 1865, at the end of the Civil War, Boynton and his son Raymond began cutting timber and floating it downstream to a newly constructed sawmill at Choctawhatchee Bay. Boynton became known as a gregarious sort who enjoyed playing the fiddle at the dances he hosted in his home. The music is said to have wafted as far away as the logging camps, and it was not uncommon for these men to join in on the frolics.

According to Dale Cox, author of *Two Eggs, Florida: A collection of Ghost Stories, Legends and Unusual Facts*, the music and good times did not end with the death of Moses Boynton. His house stood abandoned for a long period thereafter, but for many years, people passing by the old place claimed to have heard the unmistakable sounds of laughter, dancing feet and rousing fiddle music. Eventually, the dilapidated old house either fell down on its own or was pulled down. Now that the timber industry has left the area, no one really enters the area where Moses Boynton's house once stood. Author Dale Cox surmises that this could be the primary reason why reports of ghostly fiddling music coming from the site of Moses Boynton's house have ceased altogether.

12

WEWAHITCHKA

THE OLD GULF COUNTY COURTHOUSE

Wewahitchka, a small town in Gulf County, Florida, is typical of many small Florida towns in that its economy is largely dependent on its natural resources. Most of its citizens make their living off timberlands or farmlands. Thousands of people visit the region every year because of the Dead Lakes, which offer over eighty acres of prime freshwater fishing. The little town is also known for its Tupelo honey, which is produced in hives placed just outside the swamps and wooded areas. Honey is such an important part of Wewahitchka's image that the movie *Ulee's Gold*, starring Peter Fonda, was filmed here in 1997.

In recent years, the Old Gulf County Courthouse has brought considerable attention to Wewahitchka. Built in 1927 in the Classic Revival style, the courthouse served Gulf County until 1964, when the county seat was moved to Port St. Joe. The Old Gulf Courthouse was recognized for its architectural elegance in 1989 when it was listed in *A Guide to Florida's Historic Architecture*. The courthouse underwent extensive renovation in 1991. Today, the Old Gulf County Courthouse acts as an auxiliary to the Port St. Joe's courthouse. The old building is used as the branch office for tax collection, as the county's extension agent's office and as the Head Start office.

Although the Old Gulf County Courthouse has always been of interest to historians and students of architecture, it has just recently caught the attention of paranormal investigators. Legend has it that the old courthouse is haunted by the ghost of a sheriff who was shot and killed in the lobby. Visitors claim to have detected strange odors emanating from the basement. Some have experienced cold spots in parts of the building. A few people have reported hearing disembodied footsteps in deserted hallways. The Old Gulf County Courthouse, it seems, is much more than just an architectural gem.

WORKS CITED

BOOKS

Bradbury, Will, ed. *Into the Unknown*. Pleasantville, NY: Readers Digest Association, Inc., 1981.

Carlson, Charlie, Mark Moran, and Mark Sceurman. *Weird Florida*. New York: Sterling Publishing, 2009.

Carmer, Carl. *Stars Fell on Alabama*. Tuscaloosa: University of Alabama Press, 1985.

Carswell, E.W. *Washington, Florida's Twelfth County*. Chipley, FL: E.W. Carswell, 1991.

Cox, Dale. *The Ghost of Bellamy Bridge: 10 Ghosts & Monsters from Jackson County, Florida*. Marianna, FL: Old Kitchen Books, 2012.

————. *Two Egg, Florida: A Collection of Ghost Stories, Legends, and Unusual Facts*. CreateSpace Independent Publishing Platform, 2007.

Haskins, Lola. *Fifteen Florida Cemeteries*. Tallahassee: University Press of Florida, 2011.

WORKS CITED

Jenkins, Greg. *Chronicles of the Strange and Uncanny*. Sarasota, FL: Pineapple Press, 2010.

————. *Florida's Ghostly Legends and Haunted Folklore*, Volume 2. Sarasota, FL: Pineapple Press, 2005.

Powell, Jack. *Haunting Sunshine*. Sarasota, FL: Pineapple Press, 2001.

Watkins, Alfred. *The Old Straight Track*. New York: Abacus Little, Brown, 1988.

INTERVIEWS

Inmon, Pat. Personal interview. October 19, 2012.

Johnson, Stuart. Personal interview. October 20, 2012.

Kinnett, Ranger Mike. Personal interview. October 19, 2012.

PAMPHLETS

Avera, Troy and Gretchen. "Avera-Clarke House."

Bodick, Sue. "Gibson Inn."

The Coombs Inn. "The House that Mr. Coombs Built."

Goodwood Museum and Gardens, Inc. "Garden Guide."

VIDEO

Finn, Lillian. "The Owners of Goodwood Plantation." Margaret E. Wilson Foundation and Goodwood Museum and Gardens.

Websites

Anderson, Caryn. "Haunted Places in the Florida Panhandle." http://traveltips.usatoday.com/haunted-places-florida-panhandle-101596.html.

Avera-Clarke House Bed and Breakfast. "About Us." http://www.averaclarke.com/about.html.

Bellamy, Elizabeth Jane (Croom). "Ghost of Bellamy Bridge." http://www.rootsweb.ancestry.com/~fljackso/EJCB.html.

Big Bend Ghost Trackers. "The Allison House Inn." http://www.bigbendghosttrackers.com/ALLISONHOUSE.html.

———. "Bellamy Bridge." http://www.bigbendghosttrackers.com/BELLAMYBRIDGE.html.

———. "Daffodale House." http://www.bigbendghosttrackers.com/daffodale.html.

———. "Hanging Tree." http://www.bigbendghosttrackers.com/HANGINGTREE.html.

———. "John Denham B&B." http://www.bigbendghosttrackers.com/denhamhouse.html

———. "Oakland Cemetery." http://www.bigbendghosttrackers.com/OAKLANDCEMETERY.html.

———. "Site of 1840 Indian Massacre." http://www.bigbendghosttrackers.com/MASSACRE.html.

Carroll, Robert T. *The Skeptic's Dictionary*. "Ley Lines." http://www.skepdic.com/leylines.html.

City of Tallahassee. "Old City Cemetery: The Virtual Walking Tour—Site #4: Elizabeth Budd Graham." https://www.talgov.com/pm/OldCityCemeteryTheVirtualWalkingTourSite14Elizabet.aspx.

Clark, Allison. "Southern Spirits." http://www.gainesville.com/article/20091025/MAGAZINE01/910269984.

Cook, Patricia. "A Personal Account of the Night Ted Bundy Murdered Two Women at Florida State University." http://voices.yahoo.com/a-personal-account-night-ted-bundy-murdered-4621221.htmlo?cat=43.

Coombs House Inn. "The Coombs House Inn—A Luxury Boutique Inn Near the Beach." http://coombshouseinn.com/

Cox, Dale. "Civil War Florida." http://cilwarflorida.blogspot.com/2009/01/fort-gadsden-historic-site-sumatra.html.

———. "Fort Gadsen and the 'Negro Fort' on the Apalachicola." http://www.exploresouthernhistory.com/fortgadsen.html.

———. "The Ghost of Bellamy Bridge, Florida." www.twoeggfla.com/bellamy.html.

———. "Ghosts of the Russ House—Mariana, Florida." http://southernhistory.blogspot.com/2010/10/ghosts-of-russ-house-marianna-florida.html.

———. "Mariana's Haunted Landmark." http://www.exploresouthernhistory.com/russhouseghosts.html.

———. "The McLane Massacre of 1840." http://gadsdencountyhistory.blogspot.com/2008/11/mclane-massacre-of-1840-part-one.html.

———. "New Photos of the 'Ghost of Bellamy Bridge'—Marianna." http://flahistory.blogspot.com/2011/10/new-photos-of-ghost-of-bellamy-bridge.html.

———. "The Story of Florida's First Constitution." http://www.exploresouthernhistory.com/poststjoe4.html.

———. "Two-Toed Tom—Alligator Monster of Florida and Alabama." http://www.exploresouthernhistory.com/alligator2.html.

WORKS CITED

Cross, Jacqueline. "Hauntings of North Florida." http://suite101.com/article/Hauntings-of-north-florida-a75607.

Dickle, Merritt. "The History of the Russ House." http://www.rootsweb.ancestry.com/~fljackso/RussHouse/GhostTimesPast.html.

Dnjournal.com. "My Supernatural: A Remote Beach, a Victorian Mansion & a Ghostly Encounter." http://www.dnjournal.com/archive/lowdown/2009/dailyposts/20090817.htm.

Ebberbach, Cathy. "Daffodale Ghost Tours." http://www.roadsideamerica.com/tip/18166.

Florida State Forest Service. "Tate's Hell State Forest." http://www.floridaforestservice.com/state_forests/tates_hell.html.

Forgotten USA. "Tallahassee—Jefferson Correctional Institution." http://forgottenusa.com/haunts/FL/4856/Jefferson%20Correction1%20Institution/.

———. "Tallahassee—The Lively Building." http://forgottenusa.com/haunts/FL/4858/The%20Lively%20Building/

"Fort Gadsden and the 'Negro Fort' on the Apalachicola." http://www.exploresouthernhistory.com/fortgadsden.html.

Ghosts of America. "Sumatra." http://www.ghostsofamerica.com/3/Florida_Sumatra_ghost_sightings.html.

"The Ghost of Bellamy Bridge—Marianna, Florida." http://www.exploresouthernhistory.com/bellamy/bridge.html; http://www.exploresouthernhistory.com/bellamy/bridge2.html.

"The Ghost of the Lime Sink—Chipley, Florida." http://www.exploresouthernhistory.com/wchs3.html.

Goodwood Museum. "History." http://www.goodwoodmuseum.org/history.php.

Haunted Hospitality. "Avera Clarke House." http://fuseddimensions. blogspot.com/2010_09_01_archive.html.

———. "1872 John Denham House." http:/fuseddimensions.blogspot. com/2010/09/1872-john-denham-house.

"The Haunting of the Palmer House." http://www.hauntin.gs/The-Palmer-House_Monticello_Florida_United-States_8565.

"The Knott House." http://www.flickr.com/photos/freestone/149251586.

"Ley-lines." http://www.ancient-wisdom.co.uk/Leylines.htm.

"Meeting Oak Marker (Monticello, Florida)." http://www.flickr.com/ photos/courthouselover/5335215570/.

Monticello Opera House. http://www.monticellofloridaoperahouse.com/ history.cfm.

"Oakland Cemetery." http://www.findagrave.com/php/famous.php?page =cem&FScemeteryid=72378.

"Oakland Cemetery Tallassee." http://www.wreathsacrossamerica.org/ location/Oakland-cemetery-tallahassee/.

"Oak Lawn Cemetery." http://www.strangeusa.com/Viewlocation. aspx?id=2336.

"Old City Cemetery." http://seefloridaonline.com_tallahassee/cemetery.html.

"Orman House Historic State Park." http://www.northwest-florida-travel. com/orman-house.html.

Plummer, Mike. "Old Monticello Jail." http://www.wfsu.org/dimensions/ admin/uploads/videos/viewvideo.php?num=199.

Pritchett, Jeffery. "Ghost Hunters come to Marianna Florida to investigate the Russ House." http://www.examiner.com/article/ghost-hunters-come-to-marianna-florida-to-investigate-th...

WORKS CITED

Quincy Music Theater. "History." Http://qmt.org/history/

"The Russ House." http://www.emeraldcoastparanormalconcepts.com/The-Russ-House.html.

Southeastern Ghosts and Hauntings. http://southeasternghosts.blogspot.com/2012/10/ghost-bridge-of-bellamy-bridge-marianna.

St. Clare, Corky. "Prison: Old Leon County Jail." http://ghostlyworld.wordpress.com/2012/12/05/old-leon-county-jail/comment-page-1/

St. Johns River Water Management District. "How Sinkholes Form." http://www.sjrwmd.com/watersupply/howsinkholesform.html.

"The Story of Florida's First Constitution." http://www.exploresouthernhistory.com/portstjoe4.html.

"The Tallahassee Old City Cemetery." http://www.Flpublicarchaeology.org/blog/ncrc/2012/12/13/the-tallahassee-old-city-cemetery/.

Unsolved Mysteries. "Oakland Cemetery, Tallahassee, Florida." http://html.www.unsolvedmysteries.com/usm186084.

USA Today. "Haunted Places in the Florida Panhandle." http://traveltips.usatoday.com/haunted_places_florida_panhandle_101596.html.

U-s-history.com. "The Temperance Movement." http://www.u-s-history.com/pages/h1054.html.

Virtual Tourist. "Oalkland Cemetery." http://members.virtualtourist.com/m/p/m/le761c/.

Watson, Pamela. "Ghost Stories and Haunted Places in Northwest Florida." http://suite101.com/article/ghost-stories-and-haunted-places-in-northwest-florida-a302682.

Waymarking.com. "First—Brick School Building Constructed in Florida." http://www.waymarking.com/waymarks/WMBN9A_First_Brick_School_Building_Con...

————. "Old Jefferson County Jail." http://www.waymarking,.com/waymarks/WMBWAA_Old_Jefferson_County_Jail_Montic…

————. "The Russ House—Marianna, FL." http://www.waymarking.com/waymarks/WMBRV3_The_Russ_House_ Marianna_FL.

WCTV. "Is Jackson County's Russ House Haunted?" http://www.wctv.tv/home/headlines/Is_Jackson_Countys_Russ_House_haunted_1412347.

————. "Jefferson Correctional Institution Will Officially Stay Open." http://www.wctv.tv/home/headlines/139452108.html.

————. "Leaf Theater Haunted Tour." http://www.wctv.tv/home/headlines/33242929.html.

————. "Old Tradition Stirs Controversy in Jefferson County." http://www.wctv.tv/headlines/109077829.html.

————. "The Ted Bundy Murders." http://www.wctv.tv/home/headlines/107475869.html.

Weird U.S. "The Garden of Eden." http://www.weirdus.com/states/florida/ fabled_people_and_places/garden-of_eden/index.php.

————. "Sunland Mental History." http://www.weirdus.com/states/florida/abandoned/sunland_hospital/index.php.

————. "Tallahassee's Witch Grave." http://www.weirdus.com/states/florida/local_legends/Tallahassee_witch_grave/indexphp.local_

The White Noise Forum. "Apalachicola-Gibson Inn HWY 98." http://www.thewhitenoiseforum.com/main/view_topic.php?id=3236&forum_id=243.

Wikipedia. "Abraham K. Allison." http://en.wikipedia.org/wiki/Abraham_K._Allison.

————. "Big Bend, Florida." http://en.wikipedia.org/wiki/Big_Bend_(Florida).

———. "Florida Cracker." http://en.wikipedia.org/wiki/Florida_cracker.

———. "Forgotten Coast." https://en.wikikpedia.org/wiki/Forgotten_Coast.

———. "Old Gulf County Courthouse." http://en.wikipedia.org/wiki/Old_Gulf_County_Courthouse.

———. "Palmer House (Monticello, Florida). http://en.wikipedia.org/wiki/Palmer_House_(Monticello,_Florida)

———. "Pineywoods (cattle)." http://en.wikipedia.org/wiki/Pineywoods_(cattle).

———. "Port St. Joe, Florida." http://en.wikipedia.org/wiki/Port_St._Joe,_Florida.

———. "Tate's Hell State Forest." http://wikipedia.org/wiki/Tate's_Hell_State_Forest.

———. "Temperance Movement." http://en.wikipedia.org/wiki/Temperance_movement.

———. "Quincy Music Theatre." http://en.wikipedia.org/wiki/Quincy_Music_Theatre.

———. "St. Joseph, Florida." http://en.wikipedia.org/wiki/St._Joseph,_Florida.

———. "Sunland Hospital." http://en.wikipedia.org/wiki/Sunland_Hospital.

———. "Wewahitchka, Florida." http://en.wikipedia.org/wiki/Wewahitchka_Florida.

Woodward, A.L. "Indian Massacre in Gadsden County." http://genealogytrails.com/fla/Gadsden/1840massacre.htm.

ABOUT THE AUTHOR

D r. Alan Brown is a professor of English at the University of West Alabama. Alan has written over a dozen books on ghosts and hauntings. He is an avid history buff and deeply involved in paranormal research and investigation. He is also affiliated with the American Folklore Society, the American Ghost Society and Birmingham Paranormal Society.

Visit us at
www.historypress.net

This title is also available as an e-book.

www.ingramcontent.com/pod-product-compliance
Lightning Source LLC
Chambersburg PA
CBHW070347100426
42812CB00005B/1453